BREAKING THE RULES

111 Tips for Selling Value in the Era of Procurement

Mark Shonka & Dan Kosch

This publication is designed to provide accurate and authoritative information in regard to the subject matter covered. It is sold with the understanding that the publisher is not engaged in rendering legal, accounting, or other professional service. If legal advice or other expert assistance is required, the services of a competent professional should be sought.

ISBN 978-0-9855277-2-3

Printed in the United States of America

DEDICATION

This book is dedicated to sales professionals around the world who are committed to the value they can bring their customers and courageous enough to "Break the Rules" to make it happen!

ACKNOWLEDGMENTS

We gratefully acknowledge and express deep appreciation to the many people who have made this book possible, especially Tammy Ubl, Mike Lundborg, Scott Noble, the IMPAX team and, of course, our clients.

To our friends Dave Matlow, the Founder of IMPAX Corporation, and his wife Ann and our outstanding teammates who have built this business and delighted our clients, especially:

Mike Brown, Pat Ryan, Rick Bowlby, Tammy Ubl, Jay Carthaus, Johnna Krantz, Bill Larner, Ira Kasdan, Christopher Smith, Todd Hendries, Marilynn Gregory, Tim Shea, Arturo Cadar, Andy Paterson, Alice Kung, Benoit Ripoll, Dieter Fleiter, and Mark Wettasinghe

To our clients, who have trusted us with their most valuable asset, their sales force. In particular:

Tony Ennis, Mike Gardner, Chris Powell, Patrick Kelleher, Mike Lang, Todd Starbuck, Jen Stefanics, Peter Fruehling, David Christmas, Reg Kenney, Brian Bell, Mike Beach, Phillip Hathcock, Steve Hollinshead, Matthias Heutger, Jeff Vint, Soeren Bauer, Ed Robbins, Joe Puleo, David Fraser, Gary Jarosz, Richard Owens, Doug Stine, Bob Fidler, Brian Newton, Alfred Goh, Rob Danna, Steve Griffin, Phil Soran, Anne McKeough, Bob Skelley, Mike Samuels, Todd Thompson, Mark Quinlan, Chris Poitras, Gene Duncan, Jane Duncan, Kari Lindberg, Olof Beckman, Ned Kelly, Michelle Wolter, Lynda Ramsey, John Milazo, Dan Memmen, Dennis Jandik, Dan Larsen, John Mansfield, Traci Jensen, Jim Conroy, Jeff Wroblewski, Michael Goldstein, Nels Johnson, Jeff Lindgren, Tony Dale, Jim Ford, Colleen Shanahan, Sara Sampson, Terry Mundt, Steve Larson, Neil Covaleski, Steve Hershkowitz, Jack Gaido, Chris Sutherland, Eileen Woods, Tom Orr, Eric Bevevino, Tom Kazar, Mark Hein, Kevin Roberg, Jeff Chester, Dan Wohletz, James Chenier, Bill McCaddon, Todd Gunter, Tony Pape, Brad Solensky, Brad Perry, Jeffrey Fina, Susan Hawkins, Scott McMeekin, John Arcario, Reiner Beste, John Dale, Johann Fickler,

Nick Guthier, Thomas Kaufmann, Alfred Petri, Rainer Rothfuss, Martin Toscano, Claus Wassermeyer, Dirk Hoehler, Micheal Murphy, Ralf Duessel, Richard Van Sleet, Susan Wilcox, Randy Bull, and Rick Sova

From Mark:

To Sara, my best friend and soul mate. You make everything in my life so much better and I am incredibly lucky to be your husband

To my kids, Taylor, Brittany and Derek – I am so proud of each of you and love being your dad (httsadtts)

To Katie, Karly, Blair and Scott – you have added so much to my life and make it so much richer

To my heroes, Mom and Dad, for your encouragement and faith

To my family: J. Scott; Chelle and John; Drew, Geri, Leo, Ivy and Sylvi; and Sister Marie Madeleine

To my extended family: Julie, Lon and the Brew family; Randy, Cyndy and the Blasier family; Don and the Dockry family, and the Schroeder/Benson family.

From Dan:

To my wife Therese – thank you for being my best friend and for sharing your life with me!

To Kristina, Matt, Laura, and Jason – you each mean so much to me and are a such a special part of my life!

To my Dad and Step-Dad, you are both in my thoughts every day.

To my Mom, for your loving support always

To my family, Debbie, Dan, Donna, Scott, Deann, Jim, Paal, Maureen, Kathy, Trish, Scott, Dan, and Kasey

To all of our friends and family members, who have always been there to support us.

To God, in thanks for our friendship, partnership, and this opportunity.

Table of Contents

Section B – Developing your Procurement Strategy

Section C – Developing your Sales Strategy

Section D – Execution

Foreword

Rules are made to be broken. We've heard this expression a thousand times. And yet, in the world of business, it is difficult not only to understand but to execute against this age-old adage. When is it OK to break the rules? When should we bend them? How often do we need to be assertive enough to change, clarify or even amend the rules? Who makes these rules we are supposed to break? Who has the right to ignore them? And, what rules are we talking about, anyway?

In my many years in business—all spent with value-leading organizations—one thing is most certainly clear: We do not have the luxury of simply following the rules and doing what procurement teams expect us to do, or we will lose time and time again.

But, if rules are really meant to be broken, why is it so difficult to break them in the world of sales?

With all of the attention the procurement function is receiving today, one could easily—and falsely—believe they have all of the power in purchasing decisions. This simply isn't the case. Procurement teams want you to think they have all of the control and decision-making authority, but they do not. There are still executive decision makers who are more focused on creating value than cutting costs.

Sometimes, breaking the rules is the only way to guarantee even a chance at winning the business.

Let's take a traditional Request for Proposal (RFP) as an example. How many of us—as sales leaders, salespeople or executive leaders within our businesses—agree to respond to RFPs thinking and hoping that our solution, our pricing, our proposal, our company's reputation will be enough for us to advance to the next round or even win the business? Even in situations where we've been told we aren't "allowed" to talk with the customer at all—to clarify their needs, better understand their business drivers or discuss the impetus for a needed change.

So we respond to the RFP and hope we advance. Well, ladies and gentlemen, it is simply ludicrous to think we can win business by hoping. It just doesn't work that way. As Mark and Dan's first book, <u>Beyond Selling Value</u>, so artfully pointed out: We must avoid the vendor trap at all costs, and we are fools if we think hoping is a viable strategy when trying to do so. We must build coach relationships, gain access to the actual decision makers, and present the business fit that can and will exist between the two companies. Said another way, we have to get credit for the value we bring to the table and create competitive advantage accordingly.

What made <u>Beyond Selling Value</u> so powerful was the balance between their proven process of selling value and the myriad of tactics they offered. I know the power of Mark and Dan's process and tactics because my teams around the world have implemented them to great success.

In their next book, Shonka and Kosch challenge us even more by focusing on all of these rules and sharing with us how to go about breaking them: artfully, ethically and respectfully. Done well, we can even make allies of procurement leaders along the way.

After collaborating with IMPAX for more than seven years, I know with certainty that I don't want our teams playing by the rules. We can't afford to. At senior levels, our customers expect us to be thought leaders and innovators; they want us to develop new solutions for their supply chains; and they want us to help them take their businesses to the next level, locally and globally.

They want and need us to help drive value to the bottom line. They do not want us stuck in endless processes designed to make every supplier compete on price. They need us to aspire to "trusted advisor" status within their organizations. Companies that strive to achieve this trusted advisor status must answer the following questions:

> *How do we gain a powerful understanding of our customer's business?*
>
> *Why do we merit a premium for our services?*
>
> *How do we build a relationship beyond Procurement?*
>
> *How do we sell value to people who can buy it?*
>
> *How do we demonstrate the value we deliver?*

It is nearly impossible to answer these questions while following rules designed to drive apples-to-apples comparisons.

When we understand our customers well enough to have strategic conversations with them about their business needs and objectives, we gain the confidence to drastically shift our thinking about procurement rules and processes. Sure, there is a place and a time for those procurement rules. But not for our teams—not in today's markets.

We're working with our customers to bring them transformational supply chain concepts, and to become true business resources they can count on. This strategic approach to selling is completely at odds with procurement rules and processes that almost certainly guarantee us to lose. And, we have already determined that we want to and have to win.

In <u>Breaking the Rules</u>, Shonka and Kosch do it again: offering a proven process and a series of tactics you can start implementing immediately. This is not theory. You can use it right now to sell your value in this brutal age of commoditization. I know because our team uses these ideas every day.

Break the rules. You will be glad you did.

William F. Meahl, Chief Commercial Officer
DHL

Introduction

RFPs, Internet auctions and purchasing consultants—these all are tools of the ever-powerful CPO (Chief Procurement Officer). The procurement rules are well laid out and familiar: Here is the information we want you to know; respond to these questions; follow this format; email your response by the deadline; don't call anyone else; wait to hear if you made the cut; etc.

These tools are designed to level the playing field, equalize various vendors and boil down many decisions to product and price—and they've proven very effective. This is not good for value-leading sales organizations, however, that can't afford to win based on the lowest price (or may not have the most function-rich solution at every point in time).

Previously, we published the popular _Beyond Selling Value: A Proven Process to Avoid the Vendor Trap_.

This book introduced many people to the IMPAX process, which describes how to sell value by understanding your customer's business and needs; leverages that knowledge to gain access to the real decision makers while selling effectively at all levels; and provides a format for presenting to decision makers the business and solution fit you provide—all in a compelling manner! At the heart of the IMPAX process is the question: How do customers perceive your value?

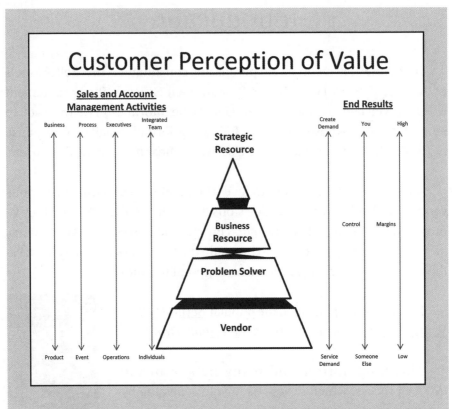

The Customer Perception of Value slide above describes the ascending levels of value sales organizations offer their customers. The more time you spend focusing on product, events, operational issues, and meeting with technical individuals and product evaluators, the lower you and your company are perceived on the pyramid. But the more your time is driven by a process that focuses on both the customer's business as well as product needs and you meet with senior-level management as well as technical and operations people, the higher you and your company will be perceived on the pyramid. You create demand because executives value you as an integral part of their business and processes.

The IMPAX process is timeless—proven over and over again. We pulled together the things effective value-oriented sales professional do by instinct into a powerful process that allows these things to be done consistently and by design.

We are often asked, "What are the biggest changes in the sales arena over the last several years?" The answer is simple: the rise of Procurement, which, in many organizations, has moved into a much more powerful and visible role.

All too often, the new procurement rules are being created so that value leaders lose. After all, the business value we can help drive doesn't always translate well to a vendor grid.

IMPAX MAXIM

"The rules are written so that value leaders lose."

We don't want to paint Procurement solely as an enemy. We all have developed good, collaborative relationships with this group. However, in too many cases they have assumed the role of gatekeeper and have marginalized the value we bring to the table. We certainly don't want an adversarial relationship. We prefer a professional, company-to-company relationship where Procurement is one of the key players. By building a beneficial and respectful rapport, we are in a much stronger position.

Sometimes it's easy to do this. In many cases, however, Procurement is going to school and learning how to better commoditize us. If we stand still while they get better, we'll end up stuck.

Combine this development of Procurement with a sales environment that is immersed in a struggling economy, competitors who are desperate and customers that are well informed and you could easily say, "This isn't your father's sales job!" Some of our long-held beliefs are now out of date. For instance, the old adage "People buy from people they like" has been replaced with "People buy from people they like when they can. Otherwise, they buy from whoever they have to."

It's clear the procurement landscape has changed rapidly and dramatically. Has the sales profession changed as quickly or as much?

Here is a challenging procurement-driven situation a client found themselves in: They were pursuing a new customer in the Canadian oil fields. It was a very complex application and they were well positioned to deliver – better than anyone else in their industry. In addition, the stakes were high. Not only would this be a huge customer with a long-term contract, but it would give them an entry point in a growing market.

So far so good. The customer decides to issue an RFP and involves four different suppliers. Looking at the competition, our client's confidence goes up. The competitors just aren't positioned to deliver against the customer's requirements, so they decided to play the game and follow the process. Imagine their surprise when they learned they had been eliminated from the bid. The RFP administrator wanted to cut the field to three "finalists" and decided that the best thing to do was to cut the most expensive alternative. Now our client is on the outside looking in and can't believe it.

Was it time to throw in the towel? No, they felt that they had to win this deal and decided to break the rules. They used several of the strategies found later in this book.

They:

- continued their research efforts
- developed stronger coach relationships
- asked their COO to reach out to the customer's president to schedule a meeting
- got in front of the real senior level decision maker

When the COO made the phone call, he was well prepared and leveraged their knowledge of the customer to make a compelling request for a meeting. It's no surprise that the president was open to a meeting.

Now the question was, "how do we make the most of this 11th hour opportunity?" They leveraged a unique presentation format you will read more about later in the book. This presentation format focuses on the customer and the value that can be created as a result of the business relationship between the companies. Here are some of the key slides:

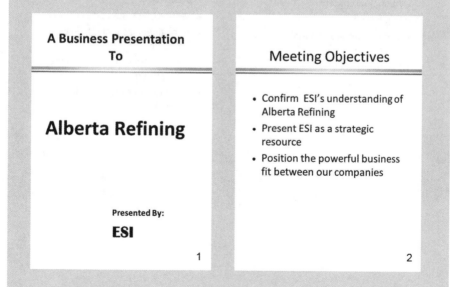

Presentation Agenda

- Alberta Refining Overview
  - Profile
  - Objectives
  - Strategies
  - Issues
- ESI – a Strategic Resource
- ESI Solution Executive Summary
- The Alberta Refining/ESI Business Fit
- Action Steps/Timetable

3

Alberta Refining - A Profile

- Market leader
- Technology and product leader
- Aboriginal commitment
- Environmental stewardship
- Safety focus
- Community commitment
- Heavy investment

4

Alberta Refining - Objectives

- Management capability
- Aboriginal content
- Innovation
- Commitment to regional leadership
- Financial results

5

Alberta Refining - Strategies

- Improve maintenance productivity
- Reduce MRO unit cost
- Re-engineer a supply chain with 7 modules
- Utilize aboriginal services in the supply chain
- Benefit from a multi-producer network

6

Alberta Refining - Business Issues

- High expectations
- Local perceptions
- Emerging competition
- Regulatory environment
- Environmental

7

ESI – A Strategic Resource

- Industry presence and experience
- Best practice leader
- Track record of innovation
- Project management discipline
- Implementation and accountability

8

The Alberta Refining/ESI Business Fit

- Builds management capability
  - Implementation plan
- Drives SCM re-engineering
  - 5 year horizon
- Utilizes aboriginal content
- Ensures innovation
  - Continuous improvement portfolio
- Supports commitment to region
  - HR plan

9

Action Steps

- Address open questions
- Ensure all Alberta Refining evaluation criteria have been met
- Provide ESI's firm commitments
- Gain Alberta Refining commitments
- Gain commitment
- Implement
-

10

After the presentation, the conversation really picked up in the roundtable discussion. It became clear that the business fit was compelling and that the companies should work together. The president made the decision based on the strategic nature of the fit and they embarked on a journey that continues years later.

Perhaps the most important point of all – they couldn't afford to lose and didn't take the "no" lying down. They would've liked to win with Procurement, but they didn't. They knew they were the best solution for the customer and they broke the rules to get back in the game. Along the way, they worked to protect their relationship with Procurement. They didn't want to hurt anyone but they had to move ahead. They had to win, and they did. **What were the key take-aways?**

- Our client did not want to hurt or offend Procurement at all
- They tried to work effectively with them but were eliminated on the basis of price
- Procurement was not going to make a decision to buy the most expensive solution, even if it was the best solution
- The client used other tactics to get to the right people and sell their value
- They probably should've done this from the start.

Fortunately, we don't have to be victims of this new reality. We can learn effective strategies, break the rules and discover where it leads. We can choose who to call, what questions to ask, how to present our response, how to react to the RFP or even if we want to respond at all.

It's completely up to us. We just need the courage and conviction to blaze our own trails. If the rules were established to make us lose, then we better not follow them. We need to make new rules. After all, there is no glory for a victim. The glory is reserved for those who find a way!

"On the road to tomorrow, are you the
windshield or the bug?"

Gary Hamill, Harvard Professor

<u>Breaking the Rules</u> is designed to give you a series of tips and ideas based on our 4-step process for selling value in the era of Procurement.

Step 1 – Assess the procurement situation to determine your best course of action.

Step 2 – Develop your procurement-oriented strategy.

Step 3 – Develop your overall sales strategy.

Step 4 – Execute your strategy professionally.

The key is having options. No idea is the correct one all the time but given enough options, we can fight back against the trend toward rampant commoditization, effectively position the value we bring—and win!

---

*"The best way to
predict the future is to create it!"*
Peter F. Drucker

Real World Application

Consider this situation faced by an IMPAX client: They received this letter from a customer when they had a successful relationship in place and three years left on their contract:

Greetings,

The University needs your assistance in dealing with an ongoing budget crisis.

...The state's revenue shortfall directly affects the University. For the first time in recent history our budget is smaller than it was the preceding year and we are in our second year of a general freeze on salaries.

Although the University has proactively cut and deferred costs across a full range of both discretionary and essential spending requirements, it is unlikely that the University can continue to absorb further cuts without significantly decreasing its expenditures to its vendors for purchased goods and services.

Accordingly, we ask that you consider providing voluntary decreases in the pricing that your firm offers to the University. We request that your firm advise us of the reduction percentage that it agrees to provide the University.

Please address our request expeditiously and advise us of your firm's intended price reduction percentage by contacting the buyer handling your commodity.

Thank you.

What would you do?

What did they do?

....

"We refused to provide proactive discounts based first on principle. We had an effective win-win relationship in place and had worked to get credit for the value we were bringing to the table. Instead of offering discounts, we went back to our coaches for additional research and insight. Next, we went to their decision maker and conducted a relationship review presentation, reflecting on the value we have created as a result of our relationship. The value in the relationship confirmed, we shared a sign of good faith by deferring their price escalation clause (which was due to kick in soon) for the following 12 months. We actually strengthened our position with the customer as a result of this procurement tactic. As a value leader, it is incumbent on us to fight for the value we bring. We cannot afford to be commoditized."

Tony Ennis
National Director of Sales
Jostens

....

Section A – Assessing the Situation

When facing RFPs, auctions and other procurement-led efforts, we have options. We don't have to blindly react and respond to the demands of the procurement process. Sometimes it's in our best interest to do just that, but other times we should run for the hills. Our time—and the time of our teammates and leaders—is valuable. It's an important part of the value we bring to any opportunity, and we have to use it wisely.

IMPAX MAXIM

"Give me a 'Yes' or a quick 'No!'"

Sometimes the procurement process is fair, giving us the access and information we need to do a good job. Other times the process isn't fair. One of the frustrating strategies we often see in Procurement is the "delay and rush". It's where the preliminary work is completed, but they just sit on it until the last minute. That's when we're expected to jump. We've waited patiently, but all of a sudden they decide it's time to act—and we need to react quickly. This tactic is used to pressure us. Unfortunately, it often works.

In order to counter tactics like this, we need to employ a thoughtful assessment of the situation and determine if and how we should respond. It may take a few minutes or a few hours, but it's well worth our time.

Tip 1. Back to the Beginning

Boating in Florida's inland waterway, a tourist capsized his boat. He could swim, but his fear of alligators kept him clinging to the overturned craft.

Spotting an old beachcomber standing on the shore, the tourist shouted, "Are there any gators around here?"

"Naw," the man hollered back, "They ain't been around for years!"

Feeling safe, the tourist started swimming leisurely toward the shore. About halfway there he asked the guy, "How'd you get rid of the gators?"

"We didn't do nothin," the beachcomber replied.

"Wow," said the tourist.

The beachcomber added, "The sharks got 'em."

This Tip takes us back to the beginning …

The most basic rule of all is who sets the rules. In most cases, the customer sets the rules and therefore has control. However, one of the best practices of talented sales professionals is that they don't let the customer set the rules or take control in the first place. Here are a few key characteristics of high performing sales professionals:

- They decide which accounts (or opportunities within existing customers) to pursue based on established selection criteria.
- If there is an RFP or auction, they determine if and how they will respond.
- No matter what they sell, they pride themselves on being a business professional who helps their customers improve their business, not on being a vendor who just sells products.

- They realize the necessity of having to understand their prospect's business and to do this, they need to conduct their research.
- They decide who to call to do this research and what questions to ask.
- They operate outside the traditional practice of calling only people who normally buy their products.
- They decide who the right senior-level decision makers are and how to meet with them.
- When determining the optimal solution for each customer, they consider not just their products and services but their company's expertise, experience, resources and relationships.
- They decide the optimal presentation flow to use when they meet with decision makers in order to make the strongest impression.
- They create an effective closing forum and determine the best way to advance the effort.
- They strive to operate proactively and even when they are reacting to a customer opportunity (as in an RFP situation), they are "strategically reactive."

In other words, they take control of the sales process and take control of their own destiny!

_____

"We are what we think. All that we are arises with our thoughts. With our thoughts, we make the world."

The Buddha

Tip 2. What are the Rules?

What are the rules and who sets them? Here is a sampling of the rules we currently see. Some of the examples might surprise you, while others might make you angry.

The customer/prospect/RFP:

- Respond to this RFP by a specific deadline.
- Give us all the required information.
- Provide us with comprehensive product and pricing information.
- Don't do additional research or contact anyone during the tender period.
- Follow the instructions of a particular consultant.
- Abide by this format for your response and finalist presentation.

In some cases, these rules (intentionally) include completely unreasonable stipulations ("The vendor will not work with any of our competitors,") to put us on the defensive and cause us to concede other points.

Our own companies:

- Follow the customer's rules, play the game and give them what they want.
- Know your products and your competition.
- Present or demo on every sales call.
- ABC: always be closing.
- Use the slide deck from marketing when presenting to a customer (you know, the 80 slides that include our logo, detailed solution overviews, photos of our people and locations ...).

Ourselves:

- Call people we're supposed to call.
- Follow their rules so we can stay in contention.
- Don't go around the gatekeeper.
- Throw enough at the wall and something might stick.
- Don't make waves.

It's not just the customer who puts us in a tough spot. Our managers and leaders can, as well—and we can even do it ourselves! In any case, we have to push back against the rules and behaviors that conspire to commoditize us.

Here's a procurement tatic that really threw one client for a loop.

"If the business leader we work with wanted to add to the scope of work with us and did so without going through Procurement, we were supposed to report the business leaders to Procurement. This left us in a precarious position between our customers and Procurement and led to the end of our work together."

Anonymous

Tip 3. Why Respond?

Why should we respond to an RFP or participate in an auction? This might seem like a simple question, but there's more here than meets the eye.

Here are some common reasons to respond:

Your pipeline is weak – Sometimes any activity in a pipeline is good. When we have little going on, it can be a relief just to have something to work on. Sadly, this is often the case even if we realize we have little chance of success. It's more about the need to feel busy than it is about being successful. On the other hand, in the absence of results, activity is the next best thing.

You feel obligated to reply – Perhaps you realize that your odds of success are pretty low, but the opportunity is with a current customer in another area—and they want you to participate. Maybe you know that the fit is weak and your odds are slim, but they don't.

Others want you to participate – Sometimes other people put us in the difficult position of feeling we need to compete even if we don't believe we can win. Perhaps a coach really wants you involved, or a teammate of yours from another division who has a relationship with the customer or one of your executives believes you should reply.

It's your organization's culture – It's your company's way. You compete hard and take your best shot at every opportunity.

You think you can win – You've assessed the opportunity and feel good about your chances. You are developing a strategy and response you think will put you over the top.

The last reason, however, is the most important one. **We should invest the time and effort in replying when we think we have a legitimate shot to win.** If we don't have a good chance of winning, maybe we should proactively pursue the right opportunities. If we feel the need to reply out of obligation, see Tip #44 "Responding, but not Really" for thoughts on submitting a partial response so you can meet the expectations but not overwhelm yourself with work.

Real World Application

Consider this situation faced by an IMPAX client:

They were pursuing their largest prospect in North America.

This was a pure prospect, and they had no business relationship in place.

An existing (and lucrative) contract was coming up for renewal.

Through their research they learned that the competitor's performance was less than stellar.

They contacted the Global Sourcing (procurement) evaluator to gain an opportunity to compete.

The Global Sourcing evaluator said, "We're just going to go ahead and renew the current contract for two more years. I am the guy who makes this decision. Call me back in a couple of years and we'll reassess whether we will go out to RFP at that time or not."

What would you do?

What did they do?

They analyzed the situation and realized they were dealing with a traditional procurement-driven gatekeeper situation. So they decided to push back hard on the gatekeeper, recognizing they had little to lose and walked through the IMPAX 4-step process for dealing with a gatekeeper (see Tip #37 "A Quote Worth Considering").

As a result of the pressure, the prospect decided to go out to bid in order to give the appearance of fairness and thoroughness. The Global Sourcing evaluator leveraged the incumbent to write the bid specs.

Realizing they had no chance to win in this context, they decided to go straight to a couple of senior level operations executives and made a presentation that demonstrated the potential business fit between the companies. The Global Sourcing contact was at the presentation and was upset. The executives, however, were excited and this gave our client the opportunity to get into two different mills with the support of senior executives.

••

"This was a tough situation. It was a great opportunity and this guy simply wanted us to lose. He wanted to continue to work with his incumbent supplier and didn't want to go through the work to upgrade his solution. If we played the game his way, we wouldn't even get a shot at the business. On the other hand, we knew that if we took a chance and broke the rules, we might just win. Of course, the gatekeeper didn't appreciate our approach, but he wasn't going to work with us anyway. The decision maker, on the other hand, bought into the potential business fit and that got us to the next phase."

Kari Lindberg
Area Vice President, Services
Metso Pulp, Paper and Power

••

Tip 4. Kicking the Tires

One of our biggest frustrations is when we lose an RFP to an incumbent and then realize the customer was never going to make a change anyway. They were determined to stick with their current supplier. If this was the case, why did they put forth the effort to administer the RFP process? There are several possible reasons, including attempting to keep their current supplier honest, to drive down the supplier's price or to justify their decision internally. Maybe they were just kicking the tires, trying to see if there was anything new out there.

Regardless of the reason, we invested a lot of time and energy—and lost. We may even feel mad at ourselves for not realizing sooner what we were up against and qualifying more effectively. If we want to avoid this pitfall in the future, what can we do?

Here are a few options to consider:

Conduct a qualifying call – Reach out to the sponsoring executive or RFP administrator and ask some questions to validate your effort (see Tip #6 "A Qualifying Call" for more ideas and specific questions to ask).

Assess the RFP – In your opinion, are they asking the right questions and looking for the information needed to make a serious decision? Are they giving you the access to information and people you need in order to submit a compelling response? Do you see this as an opportunity to be creative and innovative, or are you stuck inside the vendor trap?

Do your research – Work to understand the buying process and the role of key players. The involvement or exclusion of certain players in the organization can serve as clues to the effort's validity.

Ask a coach – Conduct your research with a coach (someone who wants you to win) to gain additional insight into the process and the people involved, the past performance of the incumbent, the level of satisfaction with the incumbent's solution and account management efforts, and the direction of the company to assess the situation and qualify effectively.

By utilizing these ideas, we should be able to more effectively qualify opportunities and spend our time where we have the best opportunity for success.

Tip 5. Apples to Oranges

Too often we see RFPs and auctions that are designed to level the playing field, so to speak, with "apples to apples" comparisons. This is particularly challenging for value leaders, as these comparisons are typically done at the lowest common denominator: price. Rarely is the focus on raising every competitor's game to the level of the value leader.

A client recently told us about a situation he faced. One of his customers went out to bid after years of working well together. The bid results were telling, as there was a significant difference in prices between the incumbent and the new competitor. The customer told our client they were going to reluctantly have to make a change, but then offered him one last chance to lower his price. Our client responded that there was no way he could provide the customer with the quality of support and the degree of attention that had been critical to their mutual success at a lower price. "How could the competitor," the customer wondered. After looking into it, he discovered that the competitor didn't have staff and all of the support would come from a call center. This was unacceptable, and the customer decided the incumbent's staff and support was well worth the additional cost.

How did this happen? Some of the bid criteria (price) were more important to the group administering the RFP than other criteria (support/ expertise), which was more important to the user.

As sales professionals, it's important for us not to get trapped in apples to apples comparisons, which eliminate the unique value we bring to the table. We must do our research, find the fit, position our value to the right people (regardless of what the evaluators think) and drive apples to oranges comparisons.

IMPAX MAXIM

"'Leveling the playing field' only works to your advantage if the rest of the competitors come down to your level. It's not good for the value leaders."

....

"We are fighting back against the apples to apples comparisons being driven by our clients and competitors that focus on the lowest cost of acquisition via a series of RFPs, pricing exercises, finalist presentations and negotiations. Instead, we are working hard to flip this upside down and drive comparisons based on the unique value we bring to the table. By helping clients increase penetration of customers, improving channels and annual order value, we create real business results, such as enhanced revenue generation and improved net income which we stand behind. We routinely work with both functional departments and sourcing and our job is to show our clients and prospects that 'best value' doesn't equal 'lowest price'."

Bob Fidler
Vice President, Sales and Client Services
Deluxe Corporation

....

Tip 6. A Qualifying Call

Sometimes we receive RFPs, and we don't know why we're included or who wants us involved. Based on the strength of our pipeline, many of us are just happy to be invited to participate, even if it means we will spend unqualified time creating an RFP response. If we haven't had input in the process and we don't know why we're included, we may want to take a different approach.

Making a call before doing any work is one strategy. Contact the RFP administrator, a procurement executive or senior-level department executive.

When you call, you will be operating from a position of strength—so consider asking these questions:

Why is this RFP being processed?

Who is the sponsoring executive?

Why was my company included?

Who else was included?

What is the decision process?

Who will make the final decision?

When will we be able to meet with the decision maker?

These types of questions—and the answers—can help us qualify an RFP more effectively from the start. One of the most important things we can gain is learning if the company will change to a different supplier if the business case is compelling. No one wants to be part of a "benchmarking exercise" or a wild goose chase.

Remember, you have nothing to lose at this point. You had no input in the process, so your odds of winning are already low. It's in your best interest to find out right away if you are column fodder—being used to drive an incumbent's price lower—or if you have a legitimate shot at landing the contract.

....

"Our selling time is an expiring asset. We have to spend our time in the best possible way and can't afford to respond for the sake of responding. We are really good at what we do and need to spend our time on deals we can actually win and get paid! It is not an order until we get paid."

Ned Kelly
VP Sales of the Americas
Arrow OCS Division

....

Tip 7. The Vendor Meeting

The vendor meeting—as part of the RFP process—is one of the most fascinating elements of the sales process. It can be informative (we can learn about the opportunity and the process) or insulting ("all you vendors come in, so we can give you marching orders").

What's our agenda for this meeting? By doing our research, we can try to determine:

Who from the customer is involved (key players, sponsoring executive, RFP administrator, consultants, etc.)?

What information is provided?

What is the opportunity?

Are they buying, or is this a fact-finding mission?

What is their buying process and what are their rules of engagement?

How will they evaluate the competitors?

What is the timing?

What type of access will be granted?

Who are our competitors?

Learning about our competition is a key factor in this meeting. What companies are involved, what representatives are present, what are they interested in, etc.? These things will help us develop our competitive strategies.

It's important we don't give away any important information about our interests and strategy during this meeting. Don't ask questions that reveal your intentions, concerns or the process you will use. Wait for one-on-one meetings before you ask any revealing questions.

IMPAX MAXIM

*"Sometimes we have a fair shot, and sometimes
we have NO shot!"*

Tip 8. Leverage Your Strength

Why were we invited to participate in a particular RFP? This is one of the most basic, yet important questions we can ask when trying to determine our strategy. There are several reasons why we might be invited:

We have coaches who want us to win – In this situation, we conduct our research with them and involve them in determining our response.

The decision maker wants us to win – When this occurs, we know we will receive an opportunity to shine at the appropriate time. We don't take this position for granted. We must do our best work in order to validate the decision maker's faith in us.

We are invited to help fill out the grid – If this is the case, then our odds of winning are low. The customer wants to demonstrate their due diligence by filling out the grid with a number of companies. A variation of this theme would include: We are invited for "benchmarking" purposes or to drive down an incumbent's price. The customer has no real intention to change, but wants to make sure they are getting the best deal possible from their current supplier. We have several options for responding to this situation, depending on what we want to accomplish.

Sometimes we are invited because we are an industry leader, and no grid is complete without our presence. If this is the case, our involvement validates their grid. Our involvement demonstrates the customer has considered all of the industry key players. If we choose not to respond, their process will be incomplete. In other words, as an industry leader, we have some power in this scenario—and we should leverage it! We can use this power to change some of the rules to our advantage and improve our odds of winning.

Tip 9. Pick Your Battles

We hear the phrase "You can't win 'em all" and of course we agree. We all have our target hit rate and with the development of sourcing strategies, such as the use of purchasing consultants and internet auctions, many of us are struggling to hit the same close ratios as before.

One of our clients told us that in a recent year, his team participated in 103 internet auctions and RFPs and only won seven of them. That ratio was well below their traditional hit rate and well below what they could afford. In addition, those seven deals were the ones they would have won if they had not participated in the bid processes at all! Our client committed a massive amount of time and effort responding to the 96 situations they didn't win.

The client learned that his team had to do a better job of picking their battles. He decided they would re-define the characteristics of a worthwhile opportunity and focus on things such as:

Do we currently have a relationship with the account?

Have we had influence on the bid specs?

Do we have a coach or coaches in place?

Can we get to the decision maker?

They ultimately decided to run hard after the right opportunities and spend the remainder of the time proactively pursuing new opportunities. The new strategy is paying off, as they are responding to fewer opportunities, increasing their overall hit rate and proactively getting involved to win deals that weren't on other competitors' radar screens.

This client's experience demonstrates that we can improve our results by picking our battles better—carefully selecting the opportunities we will reactively respond to and spending more time proactively pursuing opportunities we can win.

Tip 10. Don't Play if You Can't Win

While you weigh the concept of "picking your battles," consider doing a brief and simple assessment of each RFP using a consistent set of criteria. The emphasis is on "simple," as we don't want to get caught up in "analysis-paralysis." Below is an example of a worksheet we developed with a client to help them assess incoming RFPs:

RFP Assessment Ranking

Criteria/Weighting	Score
1. Are they a current customer? (0, 20)	
2. What is the value (size) of the opportunity? (0, 10, 20)	
3. How much effort is involved in responding? (-10, 0, 10)	
4. What is the strength of solution fit? (0, 5, 10)	
5. What is the strength of business fit? (0, 5, 10)	
6. Did we write or influence the specs? (0, 10, 25)	
7. How strong is our coach network? (0, 10, 25)	
8. Is there a consultant involved? (-10, 0, 10)	
9. Do we have access to influential players? (0, 10, 25)	
10. Can we present our response to the decision maker? (-20, 20)	
Grand Total	

See Appendix A for a blank IMPAX RFP Assessment Grid.

This is one organization's view of how best to assess opportunities. It would only take a few minutes for them to assess every RFP on a consistent point scale ranging from -40 – 175. Knowing where the score is lagging and how to improve the odds is just as important as the final score.

There are more robust and complex Opportunity Assessment tools available, but this gives a simple view of your odds of successfully competing in an RFP situation.

Tip 11. Don't Play if You Can't Win, Part 2

As you consider the previous Tip, you might think there aren't enough criteria to consider. That's OK. Just think about additional criteria that are important to you and add them. However, don't make the grid so complex that you avoid filling it out. The beauty of a tool like this is that it can make us more thoughtful—and if used correctly, more efficient. Tools like these fail when they become so complex that we avoid them or get bogged down trying to complete them.

This is a good time to remember the old K.I.S.S. adage. Here is a grid from one of our clients who uses only four criteria:

1. The strength of their solution fit;

2. The strength of their business fit;

3. Their understanding of the customer's buying process; and

4. Their ability to get to the real decision maker and present their recommendation directly.

In addition, they keep the scale of points low: the options are 0, 1 or 2 depending on their assessment of the situation. The entire point range is 0 – 8.

The beauty of this simple assessment is that there is no excuse for not doing it. The assessment only takes a few minutes, and everyone does them all the time. As a result, they have developed a strong feeling for the difference between a 0 and an 8, and they are able to do four things rather quickly:

1. Assess the situation;

2. Qualify the opportunity;

3. Identify the changes needed to win the opportunity; and

4. Speak the same language across their organization.

This is a great example of personalizing a tool, using it and driving efficiency and effectiveness.

••

"There are so many ways to waste time in the sales process, like pointless sales calls, endless demos and ineffective lunches. In sales, it's best to keep it simple. Find the solution fit, find the business fit, get to the decision maker, make your case and close. That is the fastest way to sales success!"

Brian Bell
President and Chief Operating Officer
Code 42 Software Inc.

••

Tip 12. Consider the Source

When assessing an RFP or auction, it's important to consider the source of the opportunity: the procurement department or the functional department.

This is a critical distinction for four reasons:

Qualification – The opportunity may be more qualified if the demand is coming from the functional department. It is less likely to be a tire kicking exercise if it is unfolding at the demand of a department with a need.

Contact – If it is coming from the procurement group, you are likely to be referred to procurement contacts. If it's coming from the functional department, you will most likely be referred to departmental contacts. This can make a substantial difference for value leaders who need to do their research in order to better understand and communicate the value inherent in their solution.

Depth of information – If an opportunity is generated from a department, it is likely to contain more pertinent information that will help us determine our solution and business fit. It can be frustrating when we lack the information needed to do a good job, and we can often find that Procurement may not have it either (even if they project themselves as "experts" on the issue).

Strategy – Regardless of where the opportunity originates, we need to develop our strategy in order to enhance our odds of winning. The source of the RFP has major ramifications in determining our strategy.

Tip 13. Aligning with Influence

As you assess the likelihood of winning any opportunity, your alignment with influence is an important consideration. Here are a few questions to think about:

Who is the decision maker in this opportunity?

How strong (or weak) is your relationship with the decision maker?

How strong (or weak) are your competitors' relationships with the decision maker?

Who has a position of influence in this decision?

How well (or poorly) are you aligned with people of influence?

How well (or poorly) are your competitors aligned with people of influence?

How influential are your (or your competitors') coaches?

Review this graph and plot your coaches and contacts. Where are they? If they are in the upper sections, you may be in relatively good shape, especially if they are in the upper right quadrant. If, on the other hand, they are in the lower quadrants, you may have a lot of work ahead of you and a long way to go in order to be successful. To take this even further, see if you can plot your competitors' coaches and contacts. Once it's completed, the graph will help determine your course of action.

Influence Grid

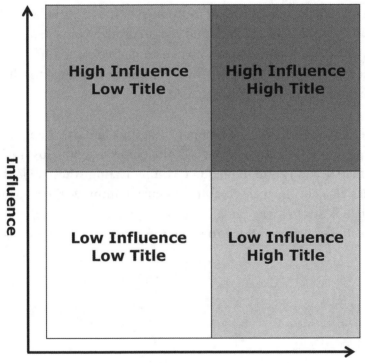

See Appendix B for a blank IMPAX Influence Grid.

Tip 14. Take it Personally

In many situations, Procurement is the highest order of gatekeeper. What's the reaction of a typical salesperson to a gatekeeper situation? One of our clients told us that "95 percent of the time my salespeople are blocked, we accept it!" He went on to say that they weren't giving up, but they were acting on faith that they could turn things around with the gatekeeper based on persistence and personality. Ultimately, it was taking them far too long to become dissatisfied enough with the situation to try something new. Sadly enough, in many cases the situations were never going to turn around, given the true motives of the gatekeepers.

Were his salespeople different from most? Probably not. Most of us believe we can wear down a block and eventually overcome it. Most of us also fear the scorned gatekeeper, who can come back to haunt us even if we are successful. The problem with this approach, however, is that it takes too much time and our odds of success are much too low.

It's better to reconsider gatekeeper situations and think about what they cost us in terms of missed forecasts, unachieved quotas, loss reviews, management scrutiny and inadequate compensation. These delays and roadblocks also cost the customer the chance to improve their business. When you look at it this way, it really affects us personally—and the sooner we realize it, the sooner we move beyond the gatekeeper.

∴∴∴∴∴∴∴∴∴∴∴∴∴∴∴∴∴∴∴∴∴

"The best sales professionals take their jobs very personally. They believe in the value of their solutions and their ability to help the customer solve their problems and drive results. Therefore, they are relentless in their pursuit of delivering that value and will not let the gatekeeper prevent them from accomplishing this task. These types of salespeople are much more likely to make the tough choice to get to the decision maker - no matter what. We need more of these types of sales professionals!"

Traci Jensen
Senior Vice President
HB Fuller Americas Adhesives

∴∴∴∴∴∴∴∴∴∴∴∴∴∴∴∴∴∴∴∴∴

∴∴∴∴∴∴∴∴∴∴∴∴∴∴∴∴∴∴∴∴∴

"Across our Strategic Accounts team, we are always trying to take dealing with gatekeepers and procurement personally. We challenge ourselves to find the right strategy for every situation we face since we have a very real and viable business value message to communicate to our customers! We have to be creative in our approach and find a way to sell that value message to the person that can buy our value!"

Jim Conroy
Director of Strategic Accounts
HB Fuller Adhesives

∴∴∴∴∴∴∴∴∴∴∴∴∴∴∴∴∴∴∴∴∴

Tip 15. Ahead of the Game

One of the best options we have for responding to an RFP is not to respond at all, but to "head them off at the pass." How do we accomplish this? By getting out ahead of an RFP and proactively selling the value and solution we bring to the table before a customer initiates the RFP buying process.

This isn't easy, however, and requires us to:

- Understand the accounts in our territory and which of them may be going out to bid in the near future.
- Do our research on the customer's business and application.
- Identify the potential decision maker.
- Design a solution (even at a high level).
- Deliver a customer-focused presentation that causes them to re-think their process.

This also requires proactive effort on our part, which isn't always easy. Many times it's easier to work reactively on identified deals—even if our odds of winning are low—than to attempt to uncover opportunities. In that case, it may be easier to work with our existing customers. On the other hand, we certainly know when our current contracts are expiring. We could decide that a few months before any contract expires, we will make proactive, high-impact, customer-focused presentations designed to extend, expand or renew these contracts. We could also leverage our good coach relationships to determine when our customers are looking at new opportunities.

When done well, we might imagine a decision maker asking himself, "Why go to all of the work in issuing and managing an RFP when we have an organization right here that knows who we are and what we need?"

Tip 16. Ahead of the Game, Part 2

In the last Tip ("Ahead of the Game"), we talked about the idea of proactively getting ahead of opportunities and presenting to decision makers before an RFP is issued. The best outcome is when a decision maker is inspired by our knowledge, solution and business fit and agrees to move forward without issuing an RFP. The worst outcome is when the decision maker starts thinking about her decision and makes a statement like, "Well, we still need to go out to bid for this."

Here are a few questions to ask when we encounter a comment like that:

What will your RFP process be?

Who will administer it?

How long will it take?

How much will that cost in terms of time and money?

What is your desired outcome?

What does it cost you not to move forward sooner?

What could this delay cost you in lost opportunities?

By asking these types of questions, we can get them thinking about the costs of issuing RFPs and the value of doing so. If we are able to engage them in an open discussion, we could also ask a more direct closing question like, **"Can we come back to you with a specific recommendation and try to earn the right to circumvent the RFP process?"**

We could also respond a bit softer with, **"You've confirmed that we have a good understanding of your direction and that there is a strong business fit between our companies. Can we propose a solution that might make the RFP process less crucial?"**

Tip 17. Bring in the Big Guns

As business development professionals, we have a variety of assets at our disposal. One of the most powerful is our own team of senior level executives. A couple of ways to leverage them are setting a strategic course and gaining support in fighting internal battles. An unfortunate reality for many of us is that we come across almost as many internal obstacles as external ones.

For instance, we see many companies that want their team to respond to each and every RFP that comes in the door. Why? For a lot of people, if a team's pipeline is weaker than desired, it can be tempting to run after almost any opportunity in order to appear busy. For some, there is a comfort level in feeling active and a degree of hope associated with even poorly qualified activity.

Although this is understandable, it can be ill advised and can easily take the life out of a business development organization. As a salesperson, there is almost nothing worse than working on an RFP or participating in an auction where you know there is little chance of success. It can be a huge waste of time, talent and energy.

It's a difficult conversation to have with a business leader when you are trying to explain that an opportunity just isn't worth pursuing and that you would like to apply your efforts to different accounts. Deciding on a course of proactive effort aimed at specific target opportunities is a difficult decision and requires executive support to help set the direction and smooth the way. Leveraging the right senior executives can make all the difference.

Tip 18. Analyze This

Dealing with Procurement is a more daunting challenge than ever before. Here's a brief exercise to help you think about your general procurement/auction/RFP response strategy.

First, what is your average win rate when responding reactively to RFPs or auctions? There are many different scenarios: You are simply column fodder filling out the grid; you are a legitimate competitor; you are the incumbent and are driving the opportunity; etc. In many cases, you are one of several respondents and hope to get to the finalist stage. Some of you have this exact data in your CRM and those of you who don't can make an educated guess.

_____%

Second, what is your win rate when you have the ability to make a traditional presentation to the decision maker? For those of you who use the IMPAX Process presentation flow of Them-Us-Fit-Action (we use the abbreviation "TUFA"), what is your hit rate?

_____%

No doubt the second number is much higher than the first. The difference is the opportunity to get off the grid and get in front of the decision maker. Now the question becomes, "What does it take to go from responding to an RFP to driving presentations to decision makers?" We need to identify the real decision maker, do our research and ask for a presentation in a compelling way. If we do this, our hit rate will go up!

"Ideas are easy. It's the execution of ideas that separate the sheep from the goats."

Sue Grafton

Real World Application

Consider this situation faced by an IMPAX client:

In the U.S., one of our most treasured holidays is Thanksgiving, which is always on the 4th Thursday in November. It is wonderful because it revolves around family and being appreciative of the many blessings we have in our lives. In millions of homes around the country, the nights before the holiday are festive, as families begin making preparations for a wonderful meal.

A client of ours received an RFP on the Wednesday afternoon before Thanksgiving.

It was a large opportunity and they were not expecting it.

One of the rules: the response was due from the vendor by Friday.

To effectively respond, it will take a team of people several hours to develop the proposal.

What would you do?

What did they do?

They responded! They were diligent, hardworking people who were trying to do the right thing and position themselves to win a big opportunity. They pulled a team of sharp people together who sacrificed much of their holiday with their loved ones in order to meet the deadline. They gave a quality response they were proud of and could position them to win—or at least get to a finalist position.

They also lost.

Of course they lost. Think about it: Were they ever going to win this? It was from a prospect, not a client. They had no input into the bid specs. They didn't even know the RFP was coming! This was never a winnable deal, and they won't make that mistake again.

....

"If there's one thing we've learned, if an RFP is a surprise to us, we're not going to win it. Maybe that's an exaggeration but we often see that a competitor has already shaped the RFP to put them in a position to win. If we get a surprise RFP, we will either decline outright or take this as an opportunity to break the rules and try a completely different approach. Based on our track record, we have nothing to lose."

Tony Dale
Senior Vice President of Sales
CPM Healthgrades

....

Section B – Developing Your Procurement Strategy

The title of this section is self explanatory. Procurement has figured out their strategy for dealing with you. Some of them, thank goodness, have decided to work with you and the user (their internal customer) to help find the best solution and a fair price. More of them, however, have decided to commoditize you, breaking your value up in parts so they can bid out the pieces.

Now it's time for us to determine our strategy for dealing with them. We have many options, and the Tips in this section are designed to help us find the right way to work with Procurement in each situation.

Have you been treated fairly and with respect by this group in the past? Great! We've got some strategies for this scenario. Have you been treated like pond scum and column fodder? Dang! We've got some ideas for that scenario, too.

"It's not your army against your enemy's army. It's your strategy against your enemy's strategy."

SunTzu, The Art of War

Tip 19. In Their Own Words

When thinking about your strategy for dealing with Procurement, consider these quotes from various procurement executives:

"We have to sell value, but we sure can't afford to buy it!" A CPO shared this with us as we worked to understand what makes him tick. The irony is that he works for one of our clients, and we are training their business development team to effectively sell their value.

"Fight for the line." This same CPO gave us this advice when we asked how we can sell our value to his company when he has made a commitment not to buy value. He went on to say that line executives in his company can choose to work with high-value suppliers, but that organizations that come through Procurement will be "put through the wringer."

"RFPs are written by someone for someone." Figuring out who is writing the RFP and who is influencing the specifications are critical tasks for us.

"In 20 years of issuing RFPs, I never issued an RFP without knowing who I wanted to win it." Wow, this is sobering, isn't it? It reminds us of the poker analogy: "If you don't know who the mark at the table is, it's you." If you don't know who the RFP was written for, it wasn't written for you!

"Understand us better!" This was the response given by a panel of CPOs at a conference when asked, "What can we as suppliers do to best serve you?" This gives us hope. It shows that at the right level they know they need us, not as simple vendors but as valuable business resources.

IMPAX MAXIM

"If an RFP isn't written by you or with you,
it probably isn't for you."

Tip 20. Know your Opponent

OK, so maybe "opponent" is too strong and too confrontational. Maybe. The fact is that now, more than ever, our solutions are being commoditized, and it is typically Procurement leading this effort. And they aren't exactly standing still. They are going to school and getting trained to be more effective at getting us to accede to their wishes and strip our value to new lows. Here are a few points taken from a training program developed to help Procurement become more effective:

- Any budget question should be countered with silence or questions about the salesperson's incentives.
- The more vendors know, the higher their profits.
- The trusted advisor role only helps the vendor.
- Ask an unreasonable amount of reasonable questions.
- Ask many questions to hide the most important items.
- Wear down the vendor and hide important items.
- Never give more information than needed.
- Ask for discounts and keep asking.
- Get the vendor's VPs and GMs involved early, as they will give you the 30 - 40% discounts and real deals.
- Their (vendor's executives) egos are involved; they will not want to lose a deal in front of their subordinates.
- Do not expose needs.
- Keep your executives away.
- Only give in on things you have predetermined not to be important.
- If they agree too early, there is still a lot of profit in the deal and you are paying too much.
- If they say it's not about the money, it's about the money.
- Never make it personal or take it personally.

This last point is a good one. It isn't personal; it's their job. Our job is to assist our clients in improving the way they do business. We can't do this if we are commoditized. If this isn't enough, think about this last point from the procurement training program, **"While working with integrity is important and developing a working relationship is appreciated, getting the best deal is most important."**

Lest you feel this is an isolated event and that Procurement really isn't learning these types of tactics, take a look at these slides from another procurement training course. Incredibly, this organization also teaches salespeople how to sell. Talk about playing both sides of the field!

7 Points for Buyer Preparation

1. Divide suppliers into: strategic, challengers, tactical and spots
2. Analyze the global contribution of each
3. Determine your importance for them
4. Accumulate all written evidence against them
5. Analyze their costs (sales forces, advertising, raw materials, etc.)
6. Set yourself a short term objective and a long term objective
7. Impose the following principle: "never go back on what we have done in the past!"

The Buyer's 10 Commandments

1. Never show your enthusiasm to a salesman
2. Always ask for the impossible
3. Always refuse an initial offer
4. Always be subordinate to someone
5. Be smart, act like an idiot!
6. Never give concessions without trade-offs
7. Always be ready to interrupt negotiations
8. Play the nice and nasty buyer
9. Take advantage of the Pareto principle (80% of concessions are achieved at the end of negotiations)
10. Never get closed in a dead end

Buyer's Training

1. Segment your portfolio of suppliers
   - Who are the strategic/tactical/challenging/spot suppliers?
   - What are their stakes for this year?
2. Analyze their contribution over a 3 year period
3. Determine your weight in their portfolio of customers, in terms of total revenue, then by product, service package, delivery costs, etc.
4. Dig out written proof of complaints/mistakes/problems experienced this year (delivery, invoicing, technical issues, customer complaints and figure out the costs incurred for your group this year) - charge to your supplier
5. Analyze improvements in the relationship (qualitative or quantitative and assess the cost incurred for the group or the economy generated for the benefit of the manufacturer.)
   - How much incremental revenue has been generated and what is our share of that?

Buyer's Training

6. Analyze the price of marketed products/services
7. Research and make the most out of your knowledge of raw material cost
8. Think about the experience curve (how experienced is your supplier) and economies of scale (how can you use your size/power to the full effect to negotiate the cost of new products/services, promotions, service charging, delivery charges, technical service, etc.)
9. With your other suppliers, assess the cost:
   - Of comparative services in line with your upcoming meeting – as a benchmark
   - Of travel expenses and accommodation/quality inspections/customer care

Buyer's Training

10. Set yourself an objective at 3 months and an objective at one year
11. To set this objective, respect the following principles:
    - Revenue of year Y is conditional for year Y+1
    - Past effort levels are recurrent
    - Recurrence should always be envisaged with a "plus"
12. Sequence your negotiation like a salami (a slice at a time to deflect your supplier, gain control, and gain concessions – PRIOR to them delivering presentation/proposal, etc.)
13. Do not negotiate alone if you don't need to, invite sympathetic/opposing colleagues to mix up the debate
14. Start with asking them for the impossible
15. Make sure they will feel uncomfortable/guilty as soon as you start the meeting

Buyer's Training

16. Claim for a concession before starting to negotiate
17. Never accept a first offer
18. Be clever: play the fool
19. Motivate them to make effort: create a carrot (a prize attractive to them)
20. Do it first and them tell them what you did
21. Be ready to stop the negotiation at any time
22. Meet his boss/present him your boss – both with specific demands
23. Behave like a pitbull – aggressive, controlled, frightening, friend, loyal, strong, winner
24. Delay any price increases proposed for at least 3 months
25. Ask for a last concession before closing

Tip 21. Do Your Homework

This Tip may seem obvious, but it's sometimes overlooked.

When determining a strategy for dealing directly with Procurement, research is one of the most important things we can do. We need to remember that, just like the sales, marketing, manufacturing or engineering departments, the procurement departments have their own unique direction—and we need to understand it.

In other words, Procurement has its own **"POSI"**:

Profile – a snapshot of where the department has been and where it is now: their mission, services, customers, culture, characteristics, etc.

Objectives – the specific goals they want to accomplish in a given timeframe.

Strategies – the initiatives the department has implemented or will be implementing in order to attain their objectives (e.g. training, technology rollout, organizational changes, etc.).

Issues – the issues that stand in the way of the department attaining their objectives.

POSI Grid

Profile (As Is)	Objectives (To Be)
Issues (Barriers & Concerns)	**Strategies** (How?)

See Appendix C for a blank IMPAX POSI Grid.

We also need to understand the formal and informal organizational structure of the department: how the organization is supposed to work and how things actually get done. It is in our best interest to know who leads the group, who are the change agents, who influences the decision maker, etc.

The information we gain about the procurement department is invaluable. If we are going to sell to them directly, we have to understand where they are at and where they are heading. If we are going to work around them, we better learn what we are up against. Nearly every Tip in this book will capitalize on effective research.

....

I am a big believer in the IMPAX Process and Beyond Selling Value, but our customers aren't always committed to buying value! We recently we faced a situation like that with one of our largest customers. Their procurement department was refusing our request for a fair price increase and instead were asking us for a deeper discount. We seemed to be heading toward a standoff that had no good outcome, where they wouldn't agree to our price and we would refuse to take their orders in the future. This standoff could mean a supply challenge for them and a big loss of revenue for us. Tensions were high so we decided to try something different. We focused on and improved our understanding of what Procurement was trying to do to support the organization's overriding goals. We used this information to clearly articulate and position our value. As they learned how we could support their efforts to address critical business issues, we were soon talking about working together to address those issues and the price became a moot point. Since then, things have changed. There is a level of trust between our companies and price is no longer the primary buying criteria. The moral of the story for us: understand Procurement's real role and interest in supporting the bigger organization's goals and position your value at every opportunity!"

Dan Wohletz
Vice President
Henkel Adhesive Technologies

....

Check out this template one of our clients uses as a standard operating procedure. They always ask for more information, which leads to better research, solutions, coach development, RFP responses—and win rates!

[Date]

[Client Name]
[Address]
[City, State Zip]

Dear [Client Name],

I have reviewed your travel services RFP in detail and am excited about the opportunity to showcase our capabilities. After careful evaluation of the information you have provided, however, I don't feel completely prepared to present the customized, value-driven solution I believe you are looking for.

Any company can offer you a list of services and their associated costs. At (our company), we strive to work closely with our customers to develop programs that are focused around your objectives. As I understand so far, your primary travel management objectives are:

[Objective one]

[Objective two]

[Objective three]

Where I need a little help is in understanding the following:

[Need more information one]

[Need more information two]

[Need more information three]

(Our company) wants your business and we are prepared to work hard to earn it – and keep it. Without additional insight into [Client Name], however, we will have to make some assumptions, which could result in less-than-optimal proposal, or possibly no RFP response at all.

So that we can put our best foot forward, I'll plan to call you [day of the week] if I don't hear from you first. Ideally, a phone conversation or short in-person meeting will be a tremendous help. Alternatively, a detailed email response could do the trick.

Your time is valuable and I thank you in advance for setting some of it aside to discuss this project with me. You won't be disappointed with what we have to offer.

Looking forward to our conversation,
[Your Name]

Tip 22. Think Ahead

Doing your research is critical and can really help to break or change the rules. An IMPAX client, who is working closely with British American Tobacco (BAT), is working hard to understand their business. Consider these comments that a senior executive from BAT shared with them:

••

"It's critical that our suppliers understand our business, but it's not nearly enough. We need suppliers who act more like partners and who understand not just where we're at now, but where we are going in the future. Our supply chain will change significantly over the next few years. Armed with this knowledge, a supplier can elevate themselves from the Vendor Trap to the level of Strategic Resource. Almost anyone can do the day to day work. These types of suppliers can help us do business better."

Bernd Meyer
Group Head of Supply Chain
British American Tobacco

••

By looking down the road, we have a chance to:

- Be more creative and insightful than our competitors.
- Proactively propose solutions that aren't even on the RFP radar yet.
- Completely change the evaluation criteria.
- Earn credibility with senior management who otherwise overlook us.
- Make a fair return on our time and services.

This futuristic viewpoint allows us to develop different solutions and more compelling value propositions than the current RFPs are asking for and to which our competitors are responding.

••••••••••••••••••••••••••••••••••••••

"We consider ourselves thought leaders and value leaders, and feel we bring superior business solutions to our customers. In order to make this happen, we have to understand our customer's business better than anyone else – where they are now and where they are going in the future. If we have this knowledge, we can create truly innovative solutions that differentiate us from the competition. This is the type of supplier we aspire to be. Without this information, we are just like everyone else, and we will be relegated to responding to RFPs."

Todd Starbuck
Executive Vice President
Business Development Europe
DHL Supply Chain

••••••••••••••••••••••••••••••••••••••

Tip 23. Ignorance is Bliss

We have the option to ignore or avoid the procurement department altogether. For many value leaders, dealing directly with Procurement is an exercise in commoditization. We know what's coming: a price-focused analysis that has nothing to do with the value we bring via our solutions and capabilities. As a result, we would rather deal directly with the department where our solution can make a difference.

When considering how we go about this, we can ask: Do we ask for permission from the procurement people or just jump into the department directly?

Remember the old adage: "It's easier to apologize for something you were never told not to do." It may be better to just jump into your sales effort with the department, being blissfully ignorant of the rules of engagement. If you were never told what they were, then there is no ill intent or personal attack on your part. You were just doing the best job you knew how to do. This is important, because if you were told by a specific individual not to do something and you do it, it can be construed as a personal affront. This is what we are trying to avoid. You want to be able to say something like, "I had no idea you felt this way. I was just doing my best to help the department."

Keep in mind that each group is different. Some procurement departments don't have the organizational power to actually block you or hurt you—while some do. This is another good reason to do research before executing your strategy.

Tip 24. Follow All the Rules

So how can a Tip under the theme of "Breaking the Rules" be titled "Follow All the Rules?" Because sometimes a great strategy is to follow all the rules and play the game as well as you can.

When might this be a good strategy? Here are several questions to consider:

Is there an incumbent?

Are you the incumbent?

Did you write the bid specs?

Did you influence the bid specs?

Did you help create the buying process?

Did you have an opportunity to lay some traps for your competitors in the specs and the process?

Do you have strong coaching?

Do you have access to the decision maker?

If the answer to some of these questions is yes, then it may make sense to follow the rules. This is especially true where you have been guaranteed a finalist presentation if you just play the game. Just make sure the guarantee comes from a reliable source.

Here's a scenario where this could be the case. An executive you've worked with in the past moves to another company. He then calls you and says he wants to do the same good work together that you've done before. Then he tells you, "We're going to work together. I just need you to help me out by building some consensus. Play the game, and I will make sure you get your shot."

Even if this is the situation, be careful how you reply to the RFP. Give them some, most or all of the information they request, but make sure you do it in a way that sets you apart and lets you position your value.

"I always say that it's about breaking the rules. But the secret of breaking the rules in a way that works is understanding what the rules are in the first place."

Rick Wakeman

Tip 25. Sell Them Well

Procurement has expectations of how we should sell to them. Often they think we should follow their rules and kiss their ring. What they want is a level playing field. What we want is anything but a level playing field. We want to tip the odds in our favor and position our superior value, so we don't have to win by having the lowest price.

These expectations are very different, so how do we bridge the gap? There are a number of ways, such as avoiding Procurement and selling to the business functions directly.

Another strategy is to sell directly to procurement, just not in the way they expect. You can utilize the IMPAX Process and "sell them well." This means doing your research on the business and also on the procurement department. Understand their objectives, strategies and issues, the organizational structure, and the identity of the key players. We then need to determine the business fit between us, the procurement department and the business function. We want to show Procurement how we can make them look good in the eyes of their customer.

In order to do this, we need to tell our story to someone who can appreciate it, in most cases a senior level procurement executive who is a business executive first and a procurement executive second. Your success with this strategy depends on your ability to find this person.

Once again we find that the best way to change someone's perspective is to sell them differently. It's not what we say that matters; it's how we act. If we don't want to be considered a vendor, then we need to exceed their expectations, earn their respect as a business resource, and convince them that we bring value above and beyond our product specs and our prices.

·······································

"When we sell to Procurement, we use the IMPAX Process just like we do with other key departments we sell into such as IT or Finance. We do our research to understand not only their needs but their direction and aim to understand not only our product fit but our business fit with procurement as well as the overall company. We also make it a priority to elevate our access to senior levels within procurement. As a matter of fact, in one instance we turned a procurement request to prepare a detailed spend analysis with our company into a strategic business presentation with procurement's leadership. We turned a potential negative into a positive and now will be meeting monthly to discuss strategic opportunities in other business areas that we were unable to get into before."

Steve Larson
Senior Vice President
Sales and Enterprise Integration Services
Enventis, a subsidiary of HickoryTech

·······································

Tip 26. Know Their Role

One of the most important things we can learn about Procurement is how they are viewed in the company. If we can learn the answers to questions like these, we will be better prepared to develop a winning strategy:

How is Procurement viewed by other people and departments in the company?

What is the official name of their function: Purchasing, Procurement, Strategic Sourcing, etc.?

Are they strategic in nature or a glorified purchasing department?

How visible are they at senior management meetings?

Do they have a CPO?

Is their CPO considered a top executive in the company?"

How visible is their mandate in the company?

How effective is Procurement at getting resources for their own use (e.g. budget for their own internal training efforts)?

Are there clashes with other functional departments in the company? Which ones? Why?

Which departments are they most closely aligned with?

At what point in the typical buying cycle does Procurement get involved?

What types of buying situations are they always involved in?

What types of buying situations are they less involved in?

By finding out the answers to these and other questions, we can form a more compelling strategy.

IMPAX MAXIM

"Keep your friends close and Procurement closer!"

Tip 27. Help Me Help You

Many of us think about Procurement as just another form of gatekeeper. If that's the case, we know we have different options on how to deal with them. One of the best gatekeeper strategies is to convert a gatekeeper into a coach, and one of the best ways to do this is to help them win. Most people win by either solving a problem or gaining recognition.

Let's look at the second idea: gaining recognition. When dealing with a procurement person or department, we might ask ourselves, "How can I make them look good?" There are no doubt a lot of ways. Here are a couple of examples:

- Is something important missing from their bid specs? What if they forgot to include something that could embarrass them down the road? By pointing it out, you can help them fix the error, avoid the embarrassment and thereby gain their appreciation.
- Are there some elements of the justification they haven't considered? Is there some element of payback they have overlooked that could impact the bid award? For example, what if they neglected to consider the impact of certain criteria on customer satisfaction? This could be so significant that it changes the eventual outcome.
- Are there opportunities to publicly recognize them and the value they have created in the process? Maybe there is an observation they made or an insight they shared that you found particularly strong. Better to share it and prop them up than to keep it to yourself.

By sharing these types of insights, you could endear yourself to the individual and gain their confidence, appreciation and loyalty. Of course, you want to make sure not to give away your competitive advantage. You have to leverage your advantages to the best of your ability. In some cases, it will involve making the procurement contact look good; and in some cases, it will involve getting credit for ourselves!

••

"We were working on an opportunity with a large customer that decided to bring in a 3rd party consultant to uncover cost savings in their processes and print buying strategies. Our team was concerned, as we weren't sure the consultant would appreciate all our integrated capabilities and would just be looking for the low-cost provider. We were concerned that we could lose all of the existing business we had. One of our Account Managers went to the consultant to learn more about what they were trying to accomplish and found out that they too were concerned because they lacked knowledge of printing, print applications and the technological developments that were impacting our industry. He educated the consultant and helped him develop a meaningful RFP, which made them look good to the customer. The consultant went on to recommend that a single source solution was probably best for the customer, and we were the only bidder who was positioned to deliver on that type of solution. We grew our business with the customer 5 times and got a contract for 5 years. This was a win-win-win situation – the consultant looked effective and credible, the customer got an efficient solution and cut their costs and we grew our business!"

Tom Orr
SVP Sales
RR Donnelley

••

Tip 28. Uncovering Value

One way to help Procurement win is to uncover something or some things they haven't considered. As an expert in your field, you have a degree of insight and experience that the procurement people most likely do not possess. Take a good, hard look at an RFP and figure out not just what they are asking but what they forgot to ask. What are they missing? If you can uncover this, you can add value to the procurement team. The win can come in different forms. Maybe it's in helping them acquire a better solution or maybe it's helping them avoid embarrassment.

Keep in mind there is a chance that one of your competitors helped them write the bid specs. If that was the case, the competitor could've left items out in order to minimize one of their weaknesses. You'll be doing the customer a favor by bringing those items to their attention, and this will position you as a potential resource for their consideration.

As you consider this idea, don't be intimidated by an interesting trend developing in procurement organizations, as they are increasingly trying to become industry or functional experts. This is taking a couple of different forms:

- Procurement people are being hired from the industry;
- People are being hired from the industry and trained in procurement practices; and
- Procurement people are being trained as experts in industry verticals or functional segments.

One of our clients faced an interesting situation like this. They received an RFP for facility maintenance and realized there was no consideration for snow removal. When they brought this to the customer's attention, they were told that it was up to them to decide whether to include it in their response. Without it, their solution and pricing were incomplete. With it, they may find themselves priced too high.

Even though they are supposedly experts, don't be tricked into thinking that somehow your value will be diminished. You have years of experience, a network of relationships and insights into best practices that can't be developed through a few classes.

Tip 29. Elevate Your Access

IMPAX MAXIM

"You can only sell value to someone who can buy it."

Whether we are dealing with a functional department or the procurement group, if we are a value leader we need to get to the senior-level decision makers: the people who can say "Yes" when everyone else says "No" and can say "No" when everyone else says "Yes." Remember, you can only sell value to someone who can buy it.

The procurement department is just like any other department: they have senior level executives (Chief Procurement Officers, not to be confused with Cheap Procurement Officers); up and coming superstars; divisive political agents; good team players; and people who are just trying to survive to the end of the day. This raises an important question for us: "Who are we interacting with?"

A couple of years ago, IMPAX sponsored a unique forum that brought together sales leaders and procurement executives. We heard from both sides and then engaged in a fascinating panel discussion. It turns out that maybe we aren't so far apart after all. But to get there it took senior level management perspective.

It seems that these CPOs are like executives everywhere. They have objectives to accomplish, strategies to implement and issues to overcome. Some are autocrats, while others try to empower their organizations. Some are right where they want to be and others want to keep moving up in the company. Most importantly, as C-level executives, they are accountable for business results. These are people who are most likely to think outside the box if it helps drive the desired business results.

If we are dealing primarily with lower-level analysts and evaluators, we are likely to feel like a vendor. These evaluators probably operate "by the book," strive for apples to apples comparisons and utilize all of the tricks in the procurement playbook. If we are dealing with executives, we may have a chance to position our value and ability to help them accomplish their objectives above and beyond the vendor matrix.

Tip 30. Pushback

In this section, we talk about having the courage and conviction to break the rules. Here is a specific example to consider:

How can we circumvent the demand of an RFP that we follow a certain process? What do we say when an evaluator tells us to fill out the RFP response and email it by the 15th of next month?

In many cases, we say "Yes!" whether or not we have a good shot to win. We could also say "No way!" OK, that sounds pretty harsh or stupid. Let's try it a different way. We can push back and ask for a different process or opportunity. We can say something like:

"Thanks for the opportunity to be involved in your process. I am excited to prepare my response, but I would like to request an opportunity to present my findings instead of mail them in. What would be a good time for me to present to the decision team?"

Does that sound too soft? How about this?

"Thanks for the opportunity. I am excited to be involved and will provide you with an excellent response. I would like to suggest a change to the process, though. I think it would be in everyone's best interest to allow me to come in and make a brief presentation overviewing our response. What is the appropriate timing for this presentation?"

How about one last variation on this theme?

"Thanks for the opportunity to be involved in your process. I am excited to respond, and my team will invest the many hours necessary to give you what you need. In exchange for this, we are asking for just one hour back from you. We'd like one hour with the decision team to present our response. What is the right timing for this presentation meeting?"

What's the worst thing that can happen? What if they still refuse and say you should just mail your response? You haven't lost anything. Now you have a clearer view of your likelihood of success and can act accordingly.

Tip 31. A Third Option

Traditionally, when responding to an RFP, we have asked ourselves: "Should we respond?" and have come up with an answer. Basically, we have had two choices. We can say "Yes" or "No." We can respond, or we can "no-bid."

In this situation, many of us have pushed ahead, following the prospect's rules and hoping to get to the finalist stage so we can earn the right to present to the decision maker and the decision team. We believe that if we can just get an opportunity to present, we can win—and we'll do whatever it takes to get there.

Now, we are trying to push this meeting up, actually getting a commitment to it as a condition of our response. This has given us a third option. Here's how it might sound:

"Yes, if …" – "Yes, we will respond if we can get a presentation scheduled with the decision maker and the decision team. What's the best way to go about scheduling this meeting?"

Or another version:

"No, unless …" – "No, we will not respond unless we are able to schedule a presentation meeting with the decision maker and the decision team. What's the best way to go about scheduling this meeting?"

These two versions are similar but different. Consider the person you will be talking to, the nature of the relationship between your company and the prospect, and the strength of your position as you determine the wording of your request. You'll want to use the right version with the right person in order for this strategy to work.

Tip 32. A Suitable Compromise

When responding to an RFP, we typically have had two choices: respond or "no-bid." These two options are not enough anymore! Throughout this section, we've shared a number of different ways to push back and change the rules. Here's another:

One strategy we can utilize is the "Compromise Strategy," where we agree to play the game as long as we get what we want. In other words, we will reply to the RFP, as long as we are guaranteed an opportunity to present to the decision maker as a part of the process. There are many different ways to say this, including:

> *"Thank you for the opportunity to compete for your business. We are excited to compete but in order for us to put in the time and effort required, we need to have an opportunity to present our response in person to Mr. Smith and the rest of the decision-making team. Our response is due on the 15th. Can we make our presentation the week before?"*

Or,

> *"Thank you for the chance to be engaged in your buying process. We are excited to compete and confident that we can earn your business. We will put in the dozens/hundreds of hours needed to give you a quality response. We just need one hour back from you in return, so that we can present our response to your decision-making team. When can we make the presentation?"*

By taking this approach, we are compromising. We are giving them what they want but in context with what we need. We will give them a response, but not until after we get a chance to present our response to the decision maker and differentiate ourselves from the competition.

Real World Application

Consider this situation faced by an IMPAX client: The new EVP of Sales received this email immediately after joining the company.

Subject: RFP - Second Chance

Dear Prospective Vendor:

We began our search for a certified supplier last year. At the October Academy, one of our Partner Physicians stopped by your booth and personally handed one of your Sales Reps a CD which contained information about our practice, a vendor screening questionnaire, and request for proposal documents. There was both a label on the CD envelope and the CD itself stated "to be considered, please complete and return RFP to Lori Johnson, Office Manager" with my contact information. The practice information document clearly stated that in order to be considered, we must have the completed information returned to me.

All four of our Partners have agreed the vendors MUST complete the questionnaire and the RFP (to the extent that the information or questions are applicable to them), and return them to me. In all but one case, Sales Reps and/or Sales Managers tried to get to the physicians rather than complying with our wishes. We will not even consider wasting our time or yours by scheduling a demo if we do not have the information necessary to assess whether or not your product will be considered in the next phase of our decision process.

It has been nearly 5 months since the doctor viewed your system and delivered our CD into the hands of someone at your booth in the Exhibit Hall. Should you wish to be considered, please kindly complete our RFP. Let me know if you have questions or concerns.

Thank you,

Lori Johnson
Office Manager

What would you do if you received this email?

What did they do?

The EVP of Sales engaged in this email exchange:

Subject: We Appreciate Your Consideration

Hello Ms. Johnson,

We are honored that you included our organization in your solution selection. As the #1 player in the industry, we are often honored with the privilege of being evaluated along with other solutions. Based on our 100% success rate, we have built the largest client-base in the industry.

Over time, we have determined that responding to blind RFPs and/or circumventing our research oriented discovery process, leads to less than optimal selection processes. In fact, our pre-sales process is a part of a continuous effort to learn about the customer workflow in order to provide the best productivity enhancing solution possible.

All of this is basically meant to convey that we respectfully decline your offer to participate in your selection process. We believe the effort will require a great deal of time and will not allow us to properly understand the important elements of your culture, strategic direction or success criteria. If you would like to vet us, we would much rather provide you a list of 10 or 15 customers that will articulate how we have helped them achieve 5% to 15% productivity gains. In fact, even if you choose to disqualify us because we are unwilling to complete your RFP, I would suggest that you demand at least 10 references from each qualifying vendor.

Thank you again for the honor of receiving your RFP. If you have any questions, please feel free to call me directly.

Michael Lang
Senior Vice President of Sales

Subject: RE: We Appreciate Your Consideration

Hi Michael,

Wow...not quite sure how to feel about this. I am shocked and impressed at the same time. You are the first vendor to give us the courtesy of a response this time rather than ignore us (or worse, promise a reply by "next week", then not deliver). You're also the only one to turn us down so graciously that I can't possibly be offended. Thank you for your time and composing such a thoughtful reply.

Having said that, I should let you know we certainly would have appreciated having received this after our first attempt back in October.

While we are not opposed to providing a prospective vendor with information about us and having a conversation to determine if we'd be a good match, we need to know our specific questions will at one point be answered. That is the only way we can determine if the solution will make it to our "short list" and be confident in our decision.

The absolute last thing I want to do is find out down the road a crucial point was skipped or a salesperson quickly talked their way past something that should have been a red flag. We want a long-term solution.

Please understand we have no interest in wasting your time with JUST the blanket RFP. We do however, use it to be certain we have the information we need and are able to make fair comparisons between the competing vendors. Of course, we would also research current user satisfaction and want input from practices as similar to us as possible. Perhaps meeting in the middle with both your pre-sales process and having our questions answered could be considered. If your team is willing, I can see how the doctors feel about a compromise.

Once again, I appreciate your time and your candor.

Lori Johnson
Office Manager

Subject: RE: We Appreciate Your Consideration

Hello Again Lori,

I actually joined in September. The RFP was received during my tenure here but it did not cross my desk. If it had been received by me, I would have responded the same way. Therefore, please accept our apology.

If we were going to compromise, my suggestion would be that we conduct our initial research, which will probably be with you and one more person. Each call should be approximately 30 minutes. After we conduct the research call, we will then present to you and your co-decision makers a 45 to 60 minute Business Fit Presentation. To ensure there isn't a misunderstanding, this will not be a demo or include any screen shots of the demo. The primary objective of this presentation is to establish a fit or lack of fit between our two organizations. However, within the presentation itself, we will agree on a roadmap for success which is embodied in the Action Items. If we agree on moving forward after this initial but very important step, I commit to completing your RFP. It will be one of the first action items.

Please feel free to call me directly. If we get through this, I will make sure I am the executive sponsor. In that role, you will have access to me throughout the process to ensure your needs are met.

Mike

Subject: RE: We Appreciate Your Consideration

Michael,

Apology accepted. I appreciate your responsiveness and willingness to address our concerns. One of our partners will be out of the office for the next 2.5 weeks, but I will arrange some time for the initial research call(s). In the meantime, would you mind sharing any reference practices you might have in the Los Angeles area?

Thanks again and have a nice weekend.

Lori

• •

"This was fun, and selling is supposed to be fun. By pushing back against their vendor-oriented process, we earned an opportunity to effectively position our value without wasting our time on an unqualified RFP response. It also showed our team that we can change the rules and still be respectful to the evaluator. In this case, we were going to lose if we responded to the RFP blindly. Instead, our strategy set the tone for a strong, win-win relationship."

Mike Lang
Senior Vice President
Healthcare Data Solutions

• •

Tip 33. No Choice in the Matter

Another strategy to consider when trying to alter the customer's RFP ground rule that demands an email response by a certain date includes telling the customer that we simply have no choice in the matter; we have to respond in person. This could sound something like:

> *"Thank you for the opportunity to participate in your process. I am excited to be involved and will provide you with an excellent response. I just have one challenge. Given my role as a Senior Client Manager, I am not allowed to simply send in my response. I have to present my response face to face with the decision team. What is the appropriate timing for this presentation?"*

This doesn't have to be dependent on the person's title; it can be a company mandate, a part of the job description or a divisional requirement. There are a lot of ways to modify this approach, but in any case it takes the responsibility for this action away from the sales rep. They don't have a choice, so they are blameless. Here's another version:

> *"Thank you for the opportunity to respond to your RFP. I am excited to be involved and confident that we can give you a powerful response. There's just one problem. My company won't allow us to send a response via email. We have to present our response face to face with the decision team. When can I make this presentation?"*

There are two ways to think about this statement. First, it might just be a ploy. Maybe it's just one more creative way to increase our odds of success by requesting an opportunity to present face to face. Second, though, what if it really is a requirement? What if we demand from ourselves and our team that, in order to do the work required to respond to a given RFP, we have to present our response in person? How assertive and compelling might we become if this is the requirement and we simply have no choice?

Tip 34. Use Your Team

There are many ways to leverage the different members of our team (IT, legal, marketing, HR, senior executives, etc.) to help us build our network and push back against the limitations that our customer's procurement organizations are routinely placing on us.

Additional assistance can come from another unlikely source: our own procurement people. These teammates can be an invaluable resource as we get their take on RFPs before we respond—and get their input on our strategy.

Another unique way to leverage them is by having them reach out, either formally or informally, to the customer's procurement people. As an example, this is an email excerpt from one of our client's procurement leaders to a customer's procurement person, in reaction to an unfavorably written RFP:

> *"After reading your RFP, I was surprised at the specifications as written. The expressed specifications differ from the specifications of the products we have provided to you for nearly a decade. Additionally, the specifications provided in the RFP appear to exclude us from consideration and directly align to another vendor's product. I am unaware of any expressed dissatisfaction for our products and am concerned by the expressed change in product specifications."*

She went on to share some specific examples of specs that were unfairly written and then said, **"In addition—we have a sustainable solution that was shown to (the decision maker) recently that does not meet any of these specifications. Are we to read from this RFP that sustainable options should not be presented if they do not adhere to the specifications?"** Then she ended with, **"Based on my understanding of the RFP, it would appear that we cannot meet specifications and should not respond. Is that an accurate assessment?"**

In one short email, she referenced the long-term relationship between the two companies, the current relationship with the decision maker and the unfairly written RFP. This may seem a little direct or confrontational, but it is just one of many strategies we can utilize as we continue to fight efforts to commoditize us.

Tip 35. Use Your Team, Again

Another way to leverage your team is to harness their capabilities to help you uncover some important information. This information focuses on past and current business relationships:

What business are we doing with the company today?

How much volume/revenue are we doing with them now and what is the trend?

What volume/revenue have we done in the past?

Which divisions, subsidiaries or alliance partners are we working with?

The answers can lead to a more powerful strategy (see Tip #73 "Quid Pro Quo"). If you've never worked with them before, maybe the questions above have less value. Another set of more creative questions includes:

Which of our strong customers are they doing business with? If we know this, we may have an additional leverage point as they seek to drive integration and efficiencies with their customers.

Which of their competitors are we doing business with? Knowing how we work (or don't work) with their competitors could provide critical clues as we formulate our strategy.

How well represented are we in their industry? The answer to this question can help us position our degree of insight and experience (if we have a strong track record in the industry) or our degree of creative and unique value (if we are not working with the other key players in the space).

The better we understand these questions, the more powerful our strategy. The answers could lead us to a stronger message, a stronger network and perhaps a stronger access strategy.

Tip 36. Focus on the Fit

One of the reasons we conduct effective research in the sales cycle is that it can help us to figure out the fit between our company and the customer. Actually, there are two different kinds of fit – the solution fit and the business fit.

The solution fit is just what it sounds like – the match between what the customer is looking for and what our solution offers. A good solution fit addresses the customer's needs and is short-term in nature. The solution fit typically appeals to evaluators and procurement people, and the focus is on capabilities and price. Most value leaders can compete effectively on the basis of capabilities, but not on the basis of price.

The business fit is different, as it speaks to how the two organizations can work together to assist the customer in achieving business objectives, implementing priority strategies, and addressing critical business issues. This type of fit appeals to senior level business executives and the focus is on the value that can be created by working together. This type of fit can be leveraged by value leaders to create a powerful competitive advantage. A good business fit leverages a strong solution fit, but includes other capabilities such as: experience, resources, expertise, networks, customer and industry knowledge and commonalities.

Both of these types of fits are important, and both have their place. Almost every salesperson understands the solution fit, and all too few really understand and leverage the business fit.

One more thing to remember – the solution fit is typically uncovered in the traditional RFP process, but the business fit almost never is. Value leaders have to create a different kind of event in the cycle to present the business fit to senior-level executives.

••

"As we work with our customers we have to focus on both the solution fit and the business fit. Of course, with medical technology, you have to make sure that the solution fits the customer's current environment and their future direction. This requires good research and coach development skills. These skills are also crucial to determining the business fit, which can set us apart from the competition by positioning our ability to impact the customer's business results. Having both together is a nearly unbeatable combination!"

Mark Quinlan
Director of Inside Sales
GE Healthcare

••

Tip 37. A Quote Worth Considering

There are numerous quotes worth remembering because of the insight they give or the reminders they provide.

"I miss 100% of the shots I never take."

Wayne Gretzky

This is a great reminder as we consider the variety of gatekeeper situations we face. It's a fact of life that salespeople and account managers will have many gatekeepers trying to block their access or strategy. Many times our first reaction can be to accept this block. It's easy to understand why. We don't want to anger the gatekeeper, we are concerned about the risk we face if we go around them, and we feel that we can convince them over time that our solution is right for them.

With the IMPAX Process, we are working to gain access to senior-level decision makers to position or reinforce the business fit between the two companies—which is tough to do when a gatekeeper is blocking us. Blindly accepting the block can be our "going out of business strategy." Instead, we recommend the following 4-step process to address a gatekeeper situation:

1. Analyze the opportunity (the upside and downside of accepting the block);

2. Understand why you are being blocked;

3. Consider alternative scenarios; and

4. Select and execute your strategy professionally.

Dealing with Gatekeepers

4. Select and Execute

1. Assess Risk and Opportunity

3. Consider Alternative Strategies

2. Understand Why

Copyright © 2013 IMPAX Corporation.

Following this 4-step process will help determine the best strategy in each situation. There is a lot at stake when we are faced with a gatekeeper. Let's not miss our shot because we never take it!

Tip 38. Getting Help from Ben Franklin

In dealing with a gatekeeper, we can get a lot of help from Ben Franklin.

No, we are not suggesting you bribe the gatekeeper with $100 bills. Instead, in accordance with Step 1 of the IMPAX 4-Step Gatekeeper Process, we are suggesting you use the analysis tool commonly referred to as a "Ben Franklin diagram" to assess the upside and downside of any gatekeeper situation. Here is a letter that Ben Franklin himself wrote explaining this idea:

To Joseph Priestley
London, September 19, 1772

Dear Sir,

In the affair of so much importance to you, wherein you ask my advice, I cannot for want of sufficient premises, advise you what to determine, but if you please I will tell you how.

When these difficult cases occur, they are difficult chiefly because while we have them under consideration all the reasons pro and con are not present to the mind at the same time; but sometimes one set present themselves, and at other times another, the first being out of sight. Hence the various purposes or inclinations that alternately prevail, and the uncertainty that perplexes us.

To get over this, my way is, to divide half a sheet of paper by a line into two columns, writing over the one pro, and over the other con. Then during three or four days consideration I put down under the different heads short hints of the different motives that at different times occur to me for or against the measure. When I have thus got them all together in one view, I endeavor to estimate their respective weights; and where I find two, one on each side, that seem equal, I strike them both out: if I find a reason pro equal to some two reasons con, I strike out the three. If I judge some two reasons con equal to some three reasons pro, I strike out the five; and thus proceeding I find at length where the balance lies; and if after a day or two of farther consideration nothing new that is of importance occurs on either side, I come to a determination accordingly.

And tho' the weight of reasons cannot be taken with the precision of algebraic quantities, yet when each is thus considered separately and comparatively, and the whole lies before me, I think I can judge better, and am less likely to take a rash step; and in fact I have found great advantage from this kind of equation, in what may be called moral or prudential algebra.

Wishing sincerely that you may determine for the best, I am ever, my dear Friend,

Yours most affectionately,
B. Franklin

It is a tool we've probably all used at different times when weighing an important issue or decision, so why not here, with one of the most important decisions we can make in our selling efforts? Most sales professionals are running and gunning and don't take the time to think this through. They often make decisions like this based on instinct or gut feeling. Here's a tool that can quickly help us think through a situation.

Simply create a T-chart. On one side, list the positives: all of the things you stand to gain if you are successful in overcoming the gatekeeper situation. Be exhaustive and capture professional and personal benefits. On the other side, list all the negatives at risk if you challenge the situation and lose. Again, be exhaustive, considering the present and the future.

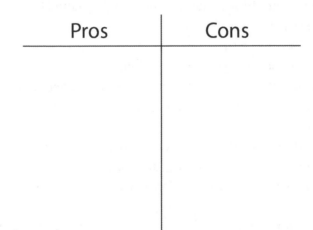

Although this isn't an exact science, just listing the pros and cons should make your situation much clearer. Do this as a first step in your gatekeeper situation, and you will be ready to move forward with something more than just instinct.

Keep in mind that there is no wrong answer. Regardless of whether your analysis leads you to say, "I'm going to sit back and accept the block for now" or "I'm going for it," you are now ahead of the game because you are making a business decision instead of an emotional decision.

Tip 39. Why?

Dealing with gatekeeper situations can be some of the most difficult challenges business development people face. Gatekeepers come in many shapes and sizes. They include customers, our own internal teammates and sometimes even ourselves. Usually, the gatekeeper is someone at our customer/prospect who is blocking our access into the account or our sales strategy and is often a procurement person.

One key to determining how to deal with a gatekeeper is to figure out why they are blocking you. There are many possible reasons, including:

- They want to maintain control;
- They are afraid you may fail and that they could look bad in the eyes of others if you do;
- They like the status quo;
- They are backing your competition;
- They feel they are simply doing their job in keeping you out;
- They are politically motivated and are rivals with your coach or coaches;
- They don't like you or your company;
- Your company fired them in the past; or
- They have had a bad experience with your company.

There are many reasons, but they seem to boil down to two types: rational or irrational. Maybe they don't know what your solution is capable of, which is a rational reason to keep you out. The rest of the reasons seem to be more irrational or emotional. It's difficult to change many of these and might not even be worth the effort to try. Most of these reasons boil down to this: They want you to lose!

In many cases, procurement gatekeepers are blocking us because it's their job. In other cases, it's because they know if they can minimize our value and save money, they can increase their own performance bonus.

Understanding the reasons why a gatekeeper is blocking us can help develop the right strategy to either convert this gatekeeper into a coach or go around the gatekeeper to greener pastures.

Real World Application

Consider the situation faced by an IMPAX client when they received this email!

Protocol for Supplier Account Executives Calling on an Account

Steve,

It just recently came to my attention that you have been contacting a number of the business unit people to possibly inquire about work already under contract with other suppliers. I am your Vendor Manager and all contact with the business units should be passed through me. This role was given to me by your former Logistics Director, and it was understood by your former President, that no one at your company would be contacting people in the businesses for sales call unless they came through me first. A direct relationship for personnel in operations has already been established through the contract and this relationship should not be expanded to include any additional work unless I am involved.

That said, please filter all request for meetings with Optimization Managers, Plant Managers, etc. though me first, with a clear definition of WHY the meeting is being requested. If it is not within my realm of responsibility as the buyer of record, I will introduce you to the appropriate buyer(s). There is a specific protocol for contract change consideration and it usually entails a competitive bid which is initiated from someone in S&L who can keep the playing field level.

I hope you understand that it is important to give all of our master contract holders equal access to any new work we may have to offer which is the reason for working through me.

Judy Smith, Procurement Manager

What would you do?

What did they do?

The rep chose to use the IMPAX 4-step process for dealing with a gatekeeper situation.

As he was trying to determine why the gatekeeper was blocking him, he believed it was because he had inadvertently overlooked her, and she felt left out.

Believing he had little to lose (as he had other coaches and relationships with decision makers elsewhere in the organization), he decided to conduct a research meeting with her. He simply asked his questions and took an interest in her perspective. She could see he was a good guy and meant her no harm. In effect, his gatekeeper strategy was to do his research and engage her in his process. By the way, he never told her that he wouldn't call on other people.

She appreciated his approach, and he left with five new contacts in her organization!

Tip 40. Face to Face

One gatekeeper strategy to consider is the face-to-face meeting. This is a high risk/high reward strategy that can be used to clarify the situation, attempt to diffuse it or even try to convert the gatekeeper into a coach.

Here are a few factors to consider when thinking about utilizing this approach:

- The strength of the gatekeeper's power;
- The nature of the gatekeeper's relationship with the decision maker;
- Their personal style: diplomatic, reserved, confrontational, etc.;
- Your personal style and your ability to keep your cool and maintain your professionalism;
- Your own savvy, the strength of your commitment and your ability to deflect an outright block; and
- The relative strength of your coach network.

The face-to-face meeting is a good strategy in a situation where you have a non-confrontational gatekeeper who may have rational reasons for blocking you. The key to a successful meeting is to focus on following the "95-5 Rule" (listening 95% of the time and talking 5% of the time), where you conduct an effective interview and get the gatekeeper talking. Find out why they feel the way they do and let them be open and honest. Don't be defensive and don't get dragged into a nasty debate. Sometimes they just need to vent or want to make sure their viewpoint is understood. Perhaps they feel left out and want to make sure they are part of the process. These issues are understandable, and you have the ability to make them feel better as a result of your meeting.

The key to this meeting is the close. You have to be able to wrap up the meeting by letting them know that you appreciate and value their perspective without giving in to their desire to block you. If you are fortunate, you may even walk out of the meeting with a new coach!

Tip 41. A Delay in the Action

As we think about our "Breaking the Rules" strategies, here's another to add to our list of options: the delay strategy.

What is this?

The delay strategy involves asking the customer for a delay (or forcing a delay if it is in our control) in order to improve our competitive position.

When should we use it?

When we are losing ground to a competitor or a no-decision and feel we are likely to lose if we continue our present course or follow the prescribed rules of engagement.

How do we do it?

We ask the customer if we can delay the timing of our response for some logical reason (availability of resources/people, logistics and schedule conflicts, the timing of a new product introduction, etc.).

What can go wrong?

The worst thing that could happen is that the customer says "No." In addition, some of our teammates or leaders might not appreciate the strategy and feel that we are foolishly jeopardizing the opportunity. In reality, if a prospect won't give us an extension, that may tell us a lot about the situation and our odds of success.

The good news?

They might say "Yes," which gives us opportunity. If they say "No," we can still choose to meet their deadline.

What do we do with the time we gained?

Use the IMPAX process: do our research, identify and leverage coaches, hone our solution fit and business fit, gain access to senior-level decision makers, involve our executives, change the ground rules and develop a more effective competitive strategy. In other words, strengthen our competitive position and improve our odds of winning.

No strategy works in every situation, and this one may be arguably less effective in a public sector environment where strict adherence to the rules of engagement is expected. Nonetheless, more options are always better than fewer options.

Tip 42. A Quick Consultation

The involvement of a consultant is a common aspect of many sales cycles, as some of our customers and prospects are hiring consultants to assist them in making specific buying decisions. These consultants range from individual industry experts to large accounting and consulting organizations, and their role typically includes developing and administering RFPs and auctions. Conventional wisdom says we need to give these consultants what they want and follow the rules.

However, we need to challenge that wisdom and consider breaking the consultant's rules. After all, we need to understand that it's in the consultant's best interest to make the buying process as complex as possible and to minimize the differences between the competitors. Our preferred strategy is to treat these players like any other key influencer in the buying cycle instead of the decision maker, and to ask ourselves key questions such as:

Who hired the consultant?

What are they trying to accomplish?

Who will act on the consultant's recommendation?

How are they being compensated (by driving vendor's prices down)?

Have we been involved with them in the past?

If so, what was our relationship, and how did they impact our success?

This last question is critical. If we have worked with them in the past and have won as a result of their involvement, we might consider them a possible coach. If we have lost, we may be more likely to consider them a gatekeeper. If they are actively restricting our access to the decision maker and others in the organization, there's no question they are gatekeepers. In any case, we have to look at the situation and treat them like any other key player. It's up to us to decide who we will work with and how we will work with them.

In the end, we can't assume consultants make these decisions or that we have to follow their rules. Our responsibility as value leaders is to understand our customer's business and needs and help them achieve success. We can't let anyone, even a paid consultant, stand in the way.

Consider this anecdote from one of our IMPAX teammates:

··

""Earlier in my career I was an Account Representative for IBM in Canada. It was an era when IBM routinely won more than our fair share of the business. Imagine our surprise when a consultant came on the scene that didn't care for IBM and consistently steered customers away from us. We worked hard to connect with this person and to help him see the value IBM could bring to the table. But he wasn't having any of it. After a year or so, when IBM lost every deal this consultant was involved with, we decided to change our approach. We would never again jump through hoops to compete when he was involved. Who could blame us? Instead, we went directly to the customer involved and explained the situation – when this consultant was involved we weren't going to win. We told them that we still wanted to try to earn their business and simply asked for the opportunity to work directly with them to give it our best shot. Almost every customer agreed to our request, and we got back on track, winning more than our fair share."

Bill Larner
IMPAX Corporation

··

Tip 43. Time is of the Essence

One of the rules we see most often calls for an all-too-speedy response to an RFP.

By the way, who is more at fault here: the prospect for demanding the ridiculous turnaround or the supplier for agreeing to the timeframe?

Why is this happening? We know they have had plenty of time to develop the RFP. Some organizations take months to develop the bid specs and the process. So why not give vendors more time to respond? In many cases, it's to keep the supplier scrambling and on the defensive.

What can we do about this? Well, we can decide what timeframe works for us and let the customer know when to expect our response. After all, we have a lot to consider: Who from our team needs to be involved, their availability, coordinating the efforts of multiple people, etc. Strangely, this would seem to be in the prospect's best interest, as well. After all, the quality of our response may easily reflect the time we have to respond.

How do we tell the customer? Just lay it out for them: "Here's what we need from a timing perspective to give you the high-quality response you deserve." If they react poorly, it's probably time to assess our overall odds of success and react accordingly.

Tip 44. Responding, but not Really

We receive many RFPs that typically contain marching orders: respond by a given time following a certain format with specified information—all designed to level the playing field. These are their rules, and we don't have to follow them.

We have lots of ways to spend our time, and we need to qualify our efforts. We need to decide if a situation is worth responding to, or what the ramifications are if we casually "no-bid". That is one of the biggest quandaries of all: balancing the time savings associated with "no-bidding" on an RFP we don't feel we'll win with the need to respond so we can stay in contention for future, more winnable opportunities. We don't want to be seen as "the company who blew them off" just before a real opportunity comes along.

Although submitting a "no-bid" is a good option in some situations, another option to consider is to submit a response that doesn't follow their format. Your response could include:

- A statement of appreciation for their consideration and the opportunity to participate;
- An executive summary that efficiently covers what you know about their business direction and solution requirements, your business and solution overview and the compelling fit that you see between the two companies; and
- A suggested set of action steps that includes a face-to-face presentation meeting with the decision maker, a more detailed proposal response and the investment/pricing information they require.

This type of response can result in a win-win scenario. You demonstrate your interest by responding in a professional way so you stay in contention on future opportunities, you don't waste too much time on a wild goose chase and if they like your response, you have helped set the rules of engagement.

Tip 45. Plan B

We see a lot of different types of RFPs in our business development efforts:

- Some that seem tailor-made for our solution and value;
- Some that seem like the customer just wants a cheap solution;
- Some that look as if the customer is just testing the waters and not sincere about making a decision or a change; and
- Some where the customer wants all of the value with none of the costs.

This last type can be especially frustrating—the fit is there but the interest in investing in value isn't. Or worse, they want the superior solution you offer but want it at a price you can't meet.

It's in these situations where we can find ourselves in a bad spot, as discussed in a previous Tip (Tip #5 "Apples to Oranges"). As sales professionals, it's important to make sure we don't get trapped in unfair comparisons where we are relegated to offering a superior solution while competing for low-cost position against inferior solutions.

Consider this strategy when responding to an RFP: provide alternative proposals. Your first proposal could be for your stripped-down solution and its associated price. The second proposal, sent completely independent of the first, could be positioned as "an alternative for your consideration." This could contain a more robust solution that you feel could provide improved outcomes and results, complete with the value positioning and investment associated with this superior solution. This proposal could whet the customer's interest and open up a dialogue on the solution and value you can bring to the table.

By using this strategy, we can compete on both an "apples to apples" and "apples to oranges" basis.

Tip 46. Plan B, Part 2

As you consider the last Tip, you may be wondering:

"If I am planning to submit an alternate Plan B proposal, is it a good idea to communicate this intent ahead of my submission to gain alignment and prevent Procurement from accidentally scoring the alternative proposal as my primary (lower cost) response?"

This is a good question and has many possible answers. Here are a few options to consider:

- We can notify Procurement ahead of time, before we submit the alternate proposals. This is risky, as they could try to "cut us off at the pass." We might want to do this only where we know the organization and feel that this will be received positively (or at least neutrally);
- We could submit versions one and two at the same time, with a positioning letter that explains our perspective and strategy; or
- We could send in the first response (the one they are expecting), then follow at the "11th hour" with the second proposal.

Any of these strategies can be effective in different situations, so you should review this situation with a good coach.

In any case, we want to positively position our strategy. A professional letter or email explaining our strategy is critical. In this letter, we should share why we are sending two separate responses. First, because we want to provide them a response that gives them what they ask. Second, that we have a proposal that can more effectively assist them in hitting their targets (we should specify a few of their key objectives, strategies or issues based on our research).

Another key question: "Who should we send this letter to?" It needs to go to Procurement, but it should also be sent to functional and business executives. After all, they are the people who are most likely to be compelled by our research, business fit and solution fit.

Tip 47. Enough is Enough

One of the rules we often see calls for an extensive overview of our company and products. As an example, a client shared this recent RFP request with us:

> "For the purposes of your response, the following information and order must be used: company information (size, financial information, market share, organizational structure, company history, safety record, etc.); company offering (technology, products and services, delivery, resources, training, continuous improvement, etc.); business partnerships (other contracts within or outside our industry, etc.); quality and delivery (standards, measures, certifications, warranties, guarantees, etc.); related business opportunities (other company offerings, affiliations, business alliances, etc.); and company organization outside the U.S. (alliances, products, services and pricing for Europe, South America, Asia, etc.)."

Huh? Are you kidding? Look at any one item in this list and imagine everything you would have to pull together. Even if you had a comprehensive proposal template, it could take hours or days to pull it all together and modify it for this response. Look at the last point: all they want is our alliances, products, services and pricing for Europe, South America and Asia! It's no wonder we're busier than ever. This was just a "first pass." Once they narrowed their list, there was more to follow.

This is a rule we need to break. We can't possibly deliver all of this. Why is this request in place at all? To narrow the list, wear us down and test our patience. Sure, maybe some of these questions are well intended, but come on. We'll burn out trying to deliver this kind of response. Our goal should be to position the value of our potential fit early and deliver only the information that is truly needed, not to go off on a wild goose chase. See other Tips (Tip # 44 "Responding, but Not Really" and Tip # 49 "To Summarize") for ideas on putting together brief but effective responses.

Tip 48. Call It Like You See It

A client told us a story that led to this Tip.

He was dealing with a large customer and received an RFP. He could tell by reading it that it was a half-hearted effort by his customer, and there was little chance any decisions or changes would be made based on the responses. Instead, the customer intended to stick with the incumbent on this piece of the business. Faced with the reality of a time-consuming RFP response for a deal he wasn't going to win, he considered his options. He decided to call the customer directly and say, "Here's what I think. This is just an exercise for you. If you simply need a number from me to fill out your grid, tell me and I'll spend a little time and get you a number. Let me know when you're serious, and I will put a win plan in place and give you a great effort and win the business." The customer conceded, our client put together a simple response, and everything played out the way it was expected.

This strategy is not right in every situation. Our client had the kind of strong working relationship that allowed him to be direct with his procurement contact. They had established an honest dialogue, and he felt he could be direct and in turn get an honest response. He also had a well-developed sense of discernment, which allowed him to be confident he wasn't passing up a great opportunity.

In the right situations, a direct strategy can save a lot of time and effort, which we can then spend on deals we actually have a chance to win.

Tip 49. To Summarize

Creating a proposal response is a critical step in most RFP situations. Often, the prospect will set the rules by spelling out exactly what they want us to include: from the required information to the specific font! After all, they want to level the playing field and break vendors down to the lowest common denominators: products and prices.

One client shared a situation with us recently where they (and every other competitor) were told to deliver only this information in their response: a company profile; their organizational structure; a detailed description of each of their offerings; a pricing schedule; and an overview of their delivery situation. Although this is a fairly standard list of items, it highlights a key challenge: How do we get our proposal to stand out when the customer demands that every respondent shares the exact same information?

We can and should deviate from the prospect's demands by including a powerful executive summary at the front end of the RFP response. Although many salespeople utilize an executive summary, all too often they are glorified solution summaries, providing a high-level solution and financial overview. We recommend a different kind of executive summary, one that highlights your value and competitive advantage.

What should this summary look like? In an upcoming Tip (Tip # 81 "Turning a Negative into a Positive"), we talk about an effective flow for a finalist presentation: "Them, Us, Fit, Action." Using this flow, we focus on:

- Reviewing our understanding of the customer's business and requirements;
- Presenting ourselves as a strategic and capable resource;
- Sharing our view of the business and solution fit between us and the prospect;
- Summarizing our proposal response; and
- Recommending a specific plan to implement.

For a powerful executive summary, why not follow this same format? You would be making your strongest possible first impression by reflecting on the customer first.

In summary, break this rule and position yourselves differently from the very start—as a business resource, not a typical vendor.

Tip 50. Special Delivery

One of the common rules we see in many RFPs pertains to our proposal response. Increasingly, we are told how our response should look, down to the specific font and its size. Incredible. The intent seems to take away any differences at all, except product specs and pricing.

This is another rule to consider breaking. Do you really want to look just like every other vendor? Do you think that if your response looks different, you will be eliminated from contention? Could it instead help you appear unique and more creative than the competition?

Here's a purchasing story worth considering, and it points out the lengths to which Procurement has gone with the RFP process. Years ago, the U.S. Air Force needed a new transport plane. They issued an RFP that had eight pages of bid specs, and Lockheed responded with a reply that was three-fourths of an inch thick, winning the bid with a plane they named Hercules. Decades later, when it was time for a replacement for Hercules, the bid specs were over 2,000 pages long. Lockheed's response weighed over three tons and was delivered via one of the Hercules planes.

Do you have a unique way to package or deliver your response? Can you use some element of your solution or capabilities to bring your response to life in a creative or interesting way? In other words, what else can you do to stand out in a crowded field?

Tip 51. Going Once, Going Twice ...

Of all the tactics used by Procurement, is anything worse than the auction? There just may be, when the auctions are blind in nature, and we don't even know whose business we are competing for. One of our clients was involved in an auction where he "won," only to find out later he was the incumbent. As he told us, "I kicked my own butt!"

As we think about a strategy, the first thing we need to ask is "Why participate at all?"

If the answer is "because we are so desperate for opportunities and have so little in our pipeline," well, good luck to you.

If the answer is because your coach or decision maker has said you are going to win the deal but they "want you to play the game," that's a viable reason.

Another reason to participate is to see what you can learn about your customer and the competitors. Go into the auction with a pre-determined price and stick to your guns. Watch and see what other people are willing to bid. Just don't fall into the trap that so many gamblers fall in to—running back to the ATM for a little more cash; or in your case, running back for a little deeper discount!

Keep in mind that the "winners" of auctions are not always awarded the bid. Check the rules at the beginning of the auction before you give anything (price, margin, competitive information, etc.) away.

A client told us about a situation where they participated in an auction with 24 other vendors. They finished at #12, and the top 15 were accepted as approved vendors. They were concerned that they had no idea how to service the customer if they were awarded business, because there was no gross profit left. They were #12. Imagine how #1 was feeling!

Tip 52. A Costly Proposition

When it comes to selling our value, especially to Procurement, we have two different battles to fight.

The first battle is "value versus cost." As value leaders, we have to use all of the tools available to us to position our value: customer knowledge and the impact we can make on their business; references; industry experience; financial return models; and projections. This is more challenging than ever—and more important! Many companies are increasingly focused on driving down costs, sometimes at the expense of higher returns. Of course, if we are going to try to win the business by focusing on value versus cost, we have to make sure we are selling the value to decision makers who can buy it. In many cases, Procurement simply isn't interested in our value.

The second battle is "unit cost versus total cost." Procurement often wants to base their decisions on unit cost. Unfortunately, unit cost measurement changes the playing field and doesn't tell the whole story. This basis of measurement slants the playing field against value leaders, who can often make an impact in other areas that may not show up in a pure unit cost analysis. Complicating this situation is the reality that, in many cases, this is how Procurement is measured and compensated: unit cost rather than overall cost. Again, it may be imperative we elevate our access to decision makers who have a different view of value and return.

What becomes clear is this: In order for a value leader to affect a decision, he may also have to affect the decision criteria and the decision team.

Tip 53. Help Set the Rules

In many of our Tips, we've talked about strategies for changing or breaking the rules. Here's a related idea: help set the rules in the first place.

How? One idea is to approach a prospect's procurement group before there is a specific opportunity on the table. In this meeting, you could do your research, learning about the practices and procedures the buying organization goes through when they initiate an opportunity. You could also share with them the processes that you like to utilize when you compete for business. Recognizing that there will often be discrepancies between how you want to sell and how they want to buy, this gives you the chance to request a compromise before there is an issue.

One advantage to this strategy is that since there is no specific opportunity on the table, there is less contention and emotion when you request a compromise. If you make a reasonable case for your ideas, there may be an opportunity to find some common ground. After all, you are not visibly challenging them in an engagement where they've already put the rules in place. At this stage, there is also less pressure on you to conform to the customer's process, and you don't have to agree to anything with which you're uncomfortable.

Of course, you can increase your odds of success in this strategy in any number of ways: utilizing your coach network, leveraging your relationship with decision makers and presenting effectively to Procurement.

What's the worst thing that can happen? The customer can say "No" to your compromise ideas, and in this case you find yourself right where you would've been anyway—but with a much clearer understanding of how the prospect does business.

Real World Application

Consider this situation faced by an IMPAX client:

The client received a demand from a prospect for a substantial up-front consulting effort to define the scope of a complex solution with no guarantee of preference or advantage. Clearly, they wanted the expertise but didn't want to pay for it.

What would you do?

What did they do?

They countered with their own significant requests. They agreed to do this on two conditions: they get regular access to the line executives, and they were guaranteed a finalist position. They created the scope, which led to the creation of the bid specs, which they steered to their advantage.

....

"Our industry is moving quickly to a services-led environment. As a result, this is an important issue for us. Sure, it's an advantage to be in the driver's seat doing the up-front consulting, but our workflow analysis consulting is significant and we deserve to be compensated for it. We are actively selling the value of this work, and charging appropriately. We've found that if a customer pays for the consulting, they are more likely to appreciate the value and give us the consideration we deserve. Of course, not everyone wants to pay for it. If the consulting results are shared with our competitors or used to write the RFP specs, we ask for access to the decision makers as a part of our compensation.

Mike Tecce
Vice President
Ricoh Global Services Americas

....

Section C – Developing Your Sales Strategy

In addition to your strategy for dealing with Procurement, you also need an overall sales strategy or attack plan. Or as one client calls it, your "win plan."

....

"It's not just about responding to what the customer asks. We have to have our win plan in place for every opportunity. Our win plan is our game plan and it aligns a pursuit team on "why and how" we will be successful. If it's good enough to spend time on, it's good enough to put a plan in place. Our win plans must be balanced – comprehensive enough to cover all of the bases, but efficient enough that we don't get bogged down. When we put a good win plan in place, we increase our odds of winning dramatically."

Patrick Kelleher
Chief Development Officer
Williams Lea

....

In the following section, we include Tips that can be used in a variety of ways and settings: with the user department, Procurement and even your own internal team. These ideas can help you implement an overall sales strategy and improve your odds of success.

IMPAX MAXIM

"You can't always differentiate yourself on product, and you don't want to differentiate yourself on price. The best competitive advantage you have is how you sell and how you do business. This is the one thing you can control every day!"

Tip 54. Develop Your Strategy

The key word in the title of this Tip is "Your." It is incumbent on today's business development professionals to be in charge of their own destiny. Part of our responsibility is to realize that our customer's procurement department has taken their game to a whole new level—investing a lot of time, money and energy to develop their strategy. They are reorganizing, using consultants, generating RFPs, conducting auctions, writing bid specs and implementing standards.

Check out this letter that was sent to one of our clients:

Valued Supplier,

My name is Julie Smith, and I joined (my company) in December to lead our world-wide procurement team. In my first 100 days, I've visited employees and business partners in each of our regions. As I continue my on-boarding, I hope to meet many of you.

I'm delighted to be here and excited about the many opportunities we have to add value by working together more effectively. One of my priorities will be to conduct a holistic review of all of our major suppliers and to ensure we are generating the optimum value from our relationship. This work will be commencing over the next few weeks.

While value includes cost efficiency and the elimination of waste, it's much more than that. Optimum value includes great service, innovation, and high quality. As we reduce costs and maximize value, (our company) remains as committed as ever to quality, where we will not compromise. In fact, we're putting even more emphasis on ensuring that our supplier base has robust quality practices and metrics.

(Our company) is focused on delivering long-term sustainable growth – growing both the top and bottom lines while continuing to invest in quality, marketing and innovation. Now more than ever, we expect our suppliers to proactively help us drive value, and we ask that you examine your business with (our company) to offer ideas on all fronts, but especially increasingly competitive costs and innovative solutions. We are also ready to change where we can benefit both you and (our company).

What does this mean? Over the coming months, we plan to:

Significantly reduce the number of suppliers across all regions and focus on those suppliers that deliver the most value. As the commodity markets have dramatically fallen over the past year, suppliers that bring us immediate pricing reductions (>10%) will be rewarded. We also plan, where appropriate, to bring new suppliers who offer value into our matrix.

Drive additional value with our suppliers. In addition, we would like to discuss what we can do jointly to remove activities that do not add value. We are aware that our processes, specifications, and requirements influence your costs and are excited to hear your ideas on what you can do differently. Those suppliers that bring substantial value to (our company) (beyond immediate pricing reductions) will do very well with us. Those that don't will ultimately not be part of our network.

Extend our payment terms. We are requesting a 50% increase in the payment terms (expect where prohibited by law) under which we currently operate. We do ask that, where the capability exists, that you invoice us electronically.

Engage with you more broadly on innovation. Let's talk about what you can uniquely bring to ensure that we continue to create products that are truly delicious for our consumers, while also leveraging health and wellness and sustainability trends. We view our suppliers' ability to innovate with us as every bit as important as delivering competitive cost and quality. We welcome hearing any ideas you may have for how we can drive greater growth.

Ensure we have a most-favored-nation clause in our contracts. As a growing global company we seek to be a core and important customer to our suppliers and anticipate that this will result in clear advantages over time – to us and to you.

You are receiving this letter because you are a vital part of our network and our long-term growth and innovation. We look to you to bring the value outlined above and will reward those suppliers that assure us a competitive advantage in this volatile marketplace.

I look forward to hearing from you soon on how you will bring immediate value to us in the areas I have outlined and many more. Please email your response no later than April 15. Or, if you prefer, contact your sourcing representative directly.

Best Regards,
Julie Smith

You really can't blame them, can you? After all, they have a lot at stake. An impartial observer might have a lot of respect for their efforts to lower their cost structure.

Well, we have a lot at stake, too. Our entire company is riding on our shoulders and will succeed to the degree we succeed. Not only that, but our customer's well-being is also at stake (if you really believe in your ability to help them improve their business).

We need to be as thoughtful and deliberate in crafting our sales strategy as our customers are in creating their procurement strategy. Too many of us operate from our "gut," going by instincts: instincts that in many cases were honed in an environment where the ground rules were different. This was before the rise of Procurement.

So let's put our own rules of engagement in place and execute our strategy. What do WE want to do, and how will we do it? Let's take our game to the next level, too!

"Strategy without tactics is the slowest route to victory. Tactics without strategy is the noise before defeat."

Sun Tzu

Real World Application

Consider this situation faced by an IMPAX client:

They were competing for an extension of a customer's business.

It was a procurement-led situation.

After responding to the RFP, the customer told them that both companies were competitive, so they decided to split the business between the two companies.

The customer also decided that the incumbent had gotten all the business so far that year, so they decided to give the next six months of business to the competitor.

What would you do?

What did they do?

They analyzed the situation and realized they had made an error dealing solely with Procurement and not the line executives.

••••••••••••••••••••••••••••••••••••

"When we learned from procurement of their decision to split the business between us and a competitor we were really disappointed. When we found out that we would get no more business until the following year we became really concerned. That's when we went to the business executive and made a presentation that focused on the strong business fit between our companies and the value we had created together. He agreed, and decided to overturn the split decision and keep working with us exclusively. That should've been our strategy from the start. We won't make that mistake again!

Jeff Park
Vice President-Builder Sales
Masco Cabinetry Groups

••••••••••••••••••••••••••••••••••••

Tip 55. Before You Get Trapped

Dealing with Procurement and responding to the rules they have put in place is a challenge. Of course, the best thing we can do is avoid getting trapped by Procurement in the first place. How do we do this? Consider these two ideas:

First, as it pertains to a prospective new customer, we can proactively position our value. This involves:

- Doing efficient and effective research;
- Identifying a compelling solution fit and business fit;
- Developing a network of coaches who want us to win and will win if we win;
- Dealing effectively with people at all levels and in different functions in the organizations;
- Gaining access to senior-level decision makers;
- Avoiding gatekeepers who attempt to block our access and our strategy; and
- Persuading these decision makers with powerful presentations that bring our value to life and differentiate us from the competition.

If we do these things, we can develop a relationship with decision makers and avoid being thrown into the trap with all of the other vendors.

See Appendix D for a sample IMPAX Business Fit Presentation designed to help us proactivley postition our value.

Second, as it pertains to existing customers, we can manage our customer relationships in a superior way. This involves:

- Continuing to do our research to understand the customer's business and degree of satisfaction with our relationship;
- Gaining an understanding of the business value we bring through our solutions, people and resources;
- Strengthening our network of coaches throughout the organization; and
- Delivering periodic relationship review presentations that highlight the value and opportunities in the relationship.

If we do these things, we can accomplish something few suppliers can effectively do: get credit for the value we bring. Once we do this, we can begin to create demand—not just respond to it—and that will help us become an indispensable business resource to the customer. Not to mention, much less likely to get thrown in the vendor trap.

See Appendix F for a sample IMPAX Business Relationship Review Presentation designed to help us manage our customer relationships in a superior way.

Tip 56. Biding Your Time

We've all done it, so let's not make any bones about it. In fact, let's turn it into a strategy. Sure, we're supposed to follow the rules, and one of those rules is to call on the evaluators and gatekeepers. After all, we don't want them to dislike us, right? Wait a minute. If we have already identified them as gatekeepers, maybe the best thing is to avoid them until we are in a stronger position. By avoiding them, we may improve our odds of either converting them into a coach or neutralizing them as it pertains to our opportunity.

If we call on them early in the cycle, we probably don't have the information, coach relationships or credibility with the decision maker we often need to turn a gatekeeper around. Avoid the gatekeeper and buy some time to do these things. Do your research and try to learn more about the gatekeeper's situation. Try to understand:

- Why they are playing the gatekeeper role;
- What suppliers they are supporting and why;
- Why they might be a gatekeeper to you;
- Their position of credibility in the organization;
- The nature of their relationship with the decision maker; and
- Who in the organization could neutralize them.

Once you've learned these things, you can further formulate your strategy. You could try to convert them into a coach, have a coach intercede on your behalf, involve them in your sales cycle or go directly to a decision maker, hoping to gain a position of strength through this relationship and your compelling business fit.

Sometimes avoiding the gatekeeper until the time is right is the best thing to do. Even if they call us on our strategy, it's easier to apologize for something we were never told not to do.

Tip 57. Issue Your Own "RFP"

In this era of commoditization, we are neither vendors nor victims. **We are business professionals who are dedicated to helping our customers improve the way they do business.** As a result, we are constantly looking for strategies that strengthen our positioning, especially in the face of increasingly challenging procurement practices.

"Destiny is not a matter of chance, but a matter of choice. It is not a thing to be waited for. It is a thing to be achieved."

William Jennings Bryant

Consider this strategy every time you think about responding to an RFP: **issue an "RFP" of your own.** This is a little different. It's not a "Request for Proposal"; it's a "Request for Presentation." By using this strategy, you are simply requesting an opportunity to present your response to the decision team. You might say, **"Thank you for the opportunity to participate in your process. We would like to deliver our response to the decision team in a brief presentation. When could we deliver this presentation?"** Notice you aren't "demanding" or "insisting"; you are simply asking.

What's the worst thing that can happen? They say "No." That's not a big deal. We've heard it before, and we've lost nothing but the few minutes it took to ask the question. We still have every option available to us: responding, elevating our access, walking away, etc.

What's the best thing that can happen? They say "Yes," and now we have the opportunity to present our response, solution and value. Think about it. What percent of the time might we get a "Yes": 20, 30 or even 50%? Whatever the exact number, it's higher than what we get if we don't ask.

Think about one last question: How will your closing rate be affected by presenting your response versus sending it in? It will be higher; the only question is by how much!

••••••••••••••••••••••••••••••••••••••

"In our organization, we have measured our effectiveness and we know what happens to our hit rate when we stand up and present – it goes through the roof. As a result, we have put a policy in place that says, 'we will not respond to an RFP without first requesting an opportunity to present our response to the decision maker.' If the customer says 'yes,' great! If they say 'no' we still have every option available to us. The reality is this – it costs us very little to improve our hit rate significantly."

Jennifer Stefanics
Senior Director of Sales Effectiveness
Exel

••••••••••••••••••••••••••••••••••••••

Tip 58. Align With the Line

Recently, in a discussion with a Chief Procurement Officer from a Fortune 500 company, we heard some terrific advice about selling value. Think about it—that's like the fox giving the hen advice on how to get out of the henhouse!

It was a fascinating situation. He was a newly-hired CPO charged with restructuring and strengthening the procurement department. At the same time, the company's sales team was one of our clients, and they were working to teach their people how to sell their value more effectively. Simply said, they wanted to buy low but couldn't afford to sell there.

He made it clear that the intent of his procurement organization was to help drive down costs in the business by purchasing goods and services at the lowest possible prices; that his people would never buy value; that they were trained to be aggressive negotiators; and that there were monetary incentives in place to reinforce this behavior. What's a value-oriented sales organization supposed to do?

His response to that question was "align with the line," meaning get out in the organization, identify business opportunities and issues, and show line leaders how you can help them conduct better business. He said, "We (Procurement) will never buy value. That's not our role. We are there to drive costs down. That doesn't mean we (the company) would never buy value. In fact, Procurement would never stand in the way of a line executive who felt they had identified the business solution they needed."

In his mind, it's up to us. We can sell to Procurement and focus on price, or we can sell to the line and focus on business value. It may not always be so simple, as we have to sell effectively at all levels; but in this era of commoditization, his advice is timely and welcome.

Tip 59. Make Your Case (TCO)

What if you can't win the price game? What can you win? This is a key question. Once you answer this question, you are then faced with "Who cares?" Seriously.

For a value leader, the area of price is one of the worst places to be able to win. Value leaders are often embarrassed when they win the business because they provided the deepest discount and have the lowest price (of course, there are exceptions to this). One of the best places to win is with TCO ("total cost of ownership"). This is a common characteristic of value leaders. Often these leaders don't have the lowest price but more than make up for it with superior quality, longer product life cycles, lower support and service costs, and rich intangibles like industry best practices that drive efficiency and throughput.

> *"Not everything that counts can be counted and not everything that can be counted counts."*
>
> William Bruce Cameron

Who cares about this? Does Procurement care about TCO? In some enlightened cases, they do. Who almost always cares about this? The CFO. If this is your competitive advantage, include them in the sales process and get them on your side. With their organizational clout, they can often override other functions if they have found a better investment that drives higher returns.

How do you compel these CFOs? You need to understand their business and metrics, and relate yourself, your company and your offering as tools that can help them accomplish their goals. Get them on your side by developing an "outside the box" financial case. You may want to consider tapping your financial leaders to help craft your TCO story, as they can be invaluable resources, offering suggestions and asking questions we may not know enough to ask.

Tip 60. Don't Trust the Specs

When responding to an RFP, we are subjected to a number of rules. Often, one of these rules limits our research-gathering activities and encourages us to rely solely on the information provided in the specs. We address a different aspect of our strategy in Tip #62, "A Rule to Ignore," where we encourage you to immediately seek some coaching and input when faced with this rule.

We want to reinforce that advice but from a different point of view.

The concern is that the information included in the bid spec isn't enough. Typically, the specs often lack context and information about the strategic and tactical direction of the organization. By the time we see the specs, the prospect has decided what products or services they need. If we lack the context of that decision, our ability to position our value and differentiate ourselves will be limited.

As an example, a client of ours was invited to participate in an RFP to help a prospect select a long distance provider. The bid spec focused on calling patterns and prices per minute, but not on the strategic direction and the real reason that a change was being made. On the surface, it seemed the primary factor was the need to drive down the price per minute of long distance services. With a little research, our client was able to learn that one of the driving forces for change was the need for a future call center application. Armed with that knowledge, our client was able to differentiate themselves by their ability to create a long-term platform that would lay the groundwork for a successful call center application while meeting current long distance needs. They were the only competitor who took this approach, and they won the deal despite having a relatively high price on long distance services.

This is just one of many examples where the information we're given may not be enough. Don't trust the bid specs—get out and do some research that can enable you to truly position your value.

• •

"We see RFPs every day, whether the person we are dealing with is in a procurement role doing formal RFPs or someone simply driving a price-only discussion. One of the things we have learned is that, in order to counter this approach, we have to do our research above and beyond the information provided in the bid specs. We sell many value-added services that can make an impact beyond that of any particular product, like a brake shoe. In order for our customer to really appreciate the value that we bring, we need to clearly articulate that value in terms of their business to the senior level people who most care about it. If we just play the price game we can't develop the kind of partnership required to be a true trusted advisor."

James Chenier
Vice President, Aftermarket Sales & Marketing
Volvo Trucks North America

• •

Tip 61. Into the Eye of the Storm

Let's say you sell widgets and are prospecting for new customers. Who do you call? Do you call the "person you're supposed to call?" You know, the person who buys widgets?

This person has been buying widgets for years, he has considered many different widget vendors, he has honed his process for buying widgets, he selected their current widget vendor six years ago, he has become personal friends with their widget supplier, he went out to bid for widgets a year ago after developing an RFP that the current widget vendor couldn't lose, and he has received a bonus based on how much money he's saved buying widgets.

This potential customer is probably getting what they think they need from their current supplier and may be reluctant to even consider a change.

What does this tell us? Does it say we can't win here or shouldn't even try? Not necessarily. We might have some capability, experience or solution this company needs, even if they don't know it yet. Of course, we have to do our research and qualify the opportunity. We have to better understand the customer's business direction and application requirements, identify our unique capabilities and determine the business fit that could exist between our companies. Then we need to compel the people who can buy our value.

This does tell us, however, that we're going to have a tough time if we only call on "the people we're supposed to call on." We better work the network and call on others, people who just may be open to coaching us and buying our value.

Tip 62. A Rule to Ignore

One of the most annoying RFP rules is the restriction on the research we can do as we prepare our response. We see RFPs that tell us:

> *"You are not allowed to make contact with anyone during this response period. If you have any questions, email them to the RFP administrator, and we will choose whether or not to answer them. If we choose to answer them, we will send our response to all of the competitors. Anyone found breaking this rule will be eliminated from consideration."*

Why do they do this? To maintain integrity? To prevent us from differentiating ourselves? To make sure we are as commoditized as possible? To keep the playing field level? All of the above?

As we know, there is no such thing as a level playing field! In fact, it's up to us to make sure that the playing field isn't level. We're in it to win it! In order to put our best foot forward, we need to differentiate ourselves. For many of us, the key to differentiating ourselves is doing the right kind of research, which we leverage in our RFP responses and presentations. We simply can't follow this rule and put our best foot forward.

As soon as we hear the "No Research Rule," we should break it. Go out to the Internet and get the data. Study it and learn more about the company than your competitors. Then, dive into your network and find someone outside the decision process to call. Even people who don't work for the company but know it well can be great sources of information and insight. Neighbors, friends, friends of neighbors, fellow salespeople ... many options are open. Remember, no one should have the right to restrict your access to people in your own network.

....

"One of my reps came to me with an RFP and told me we couldn't win it because we didn't know enough and we couldn't break the "Blackout Rule". I told her that she should break the rule and call the sponsoring executive and if she was eliminated I would pay her all of the commission as if she won the deal. She called the executive and he had no idea that the clause was even in the RFP. Nor did he care. He was happy to answer her questions because he wanted the best solution. The Blackout Rule was just in the RFP as a procurement tool. Once she broke the rule, made the call and did her research, her confidence soared and she was well positioned to compete and win!

Todd Thompson
Senior Vice President
Mode Transportation

....

Tip 63. Get Outside the Box

Don't you love buzzwords? Words and phrases like "synergy," "alignment," "organic growth," "face time," "leverage," "paradigm shift" and "empowerment." Although all meaningful, they have become caricatures of themselves. Heck, even "buzzword" has become a buzzword!

Well, one of the great buzzwords of our time is the title of this Tip: **"Get Outside the Box."** What does this mean? Although we're not sure exactly what the person who coined this phrase meant, we can relate it to many aspects of selling.

For instance, think about our search for coaches. These coaches play such a critical role in our success, yet most people find coaches in the exact same places: the people who use their solutions. Not that there's anything wrong with that!

The point is that there are many other places to look for contacts to develop into coaches: in related departments; people who have left the company; people within your own company who know the customer from past experience; other salespeople who sell to the company; friends and other business associates; retirees; people you meet at associations and trade shows; etc.

Our challenge: get creative and find coaches where others fail to look. After all, the stronger our coach network, the greater our odds of success!

Tip 64. Work the Network

How many times in a loss review have we talked about how we lost a key customer or the opportunity to win a new customer because we lost our coach? Countless times for many of us. This can be a crushing loss, and it's one of the most common reasons for losing an account or opportunity. It shouldn't be.

The problem is often found in statements like, "My coach was let go," "My coach was promoted," "My coach took a new opportunity," or "My coach went radio silent." There are a lot of variables behind these statements, but what do they all have in common? The fact that there is only one coach.

After all, what do new people who join an organization like to do? They like to bring fresh ideas or things that have worked for them in the past. If we don't have a strong network of supporters who can help us protect our position, what do we expect?

Developing a coach relationship is a great place to start, but we need to create a network of coach relationships made up of people who want us to win—and win if we win. At this point, one of the best things you can do is get a copy of their organizational chart. Look at where you have coaching and where you don't, and consider the position of the decision maker and your alignment with the people who are influential. Then get out and network with your coach to get introductions to other people. Start building the network one new contact at a time.

Developing this network is easier said than done, right? Sure, but coaches are so critical to our success, and we hate the exposure that comes with the realization that we are just a promotion or defection away from losing our best customer. Also, remember that the best way to protect ourselves from the reach of Procurement is to develop a strong network of coaches who want us to win.

••

"Developing a coach is important for our team to win. However, developing a coach network of more than one coach in different areas of the business is critical to maximizing our odds of winning and even more important in expanding our customer relationships. It could easily be our #1 strategy for successfully selling our value to the business versus being caught in the vendor trap just selling price to procurement!"

Lynda Ramsey
Vice President, Enterprise Group
Domtar

••

Tip 65. Leveraging Your Assets

One of the best tools for dealing with Procurement is often found right in front of our eyes—or sitting next to us. It is our own team. How can they help? Often, Procurement tries to keep us from infiltrating the organization and making contacts that can help us generate support and gain information. If we are blocked, what about other people on our team? Are they blocked, too?

In a recent meeting with a client's general management team, the topic of networking came up. It happens that their sales team has most of their relationships "inside the box"—the department they are "supposed to sell to"—and they need to break out. The Human Resources Director mentioned that she could help with the sales team's networking efforts. She knows a lot of HR people in their customer's and prospect's organizations and has a good rapport with them, as they routinely share HR-related strategies and ideas. The IT Director chimed in as well and talked about how he is in a number of professional associations with IT leaders from his geographical area, and that he had a number of contacts he could tap on behalf of the sales team. Then the Marketing leader contributed some of his ideas.

Of course, there is our senior management team, who always seem to be well connected with their counterparts in other organizations. As an added bonus, using our senior managers to contact the prospect's senior managers takes the heat off of us. After all, it's not our fault our executives want to meet with their executives, right?

In many cases, the members of our team are more than happy to help us, and we need to ask them. After all, nothing happens in our companies without a sale!

Tip 66. Turnabout

What happens when a coach stops coaching? Let's look at two different scenarios.

First, the quality of their coaching seems to change, and it feels like they are drifting away. They stop sharing insights, they aren't as available as they used to be, they don't seem to be sharing the quality of insights they used to share, etc. What happened here? In this case, you have to wonder if their win has faded away. Perhaps they already got what they were looking for from your relationship or decided they weren't going to get the win and have changed their views. That could explain the lack of coaching. It's not uncommon to have a coach who helps you win in one situation and is nowhere to be found in another.

Second, what if their attitudes and actions have changed significantly? What if they start saying things like, "I'll take this from here," or "The timing is bad," or "I'll let you know when you should come back," or "Let me run it up the flagpole?" This person has gone further and actually turned into a gatekeeper. We may not want to believe it, but remember: A gatekeeper is someone who blocks our access and/or our strategy. In this case, that's what's happening.

Coach relationships are just like any other relationship. They are prone to change, and we have to work to keep them fresh. In our case, we need to make sure the coach has a win when they work with us. As soon as there is no win, there likely will be no coach. Yet another good reason to develop a network of coaches instead of one coach.

Tip 67. A Way Out

When we are doing our research, one of the challenges we may face is finding new contacts to call on or finding different contacts outside our current network. Different situations can put us in this position:

- You are calling on a new prospect and trying to find anyone to begin your research with.
- You are calling on an established customer and want to expand your coach network.
- There is a gatekeeper looming on the horizon, and you want to move outside their realm of control.
- You've fallen into the trap where most of your network resides in your user community, and you want a fresh perspective.

In any case, you need someone different to call on and don't know where to go. In this situation, a great place to start is with us: fellow sales and account management professionals. After all, we are very knowledgeable about the direction our company is headed, as well as the issues our company is facing. Not only that, we are often happy to share our perspective, especially with other salespeople who are experiencing similar challenges.

If you're looking to get outside the box and develop new contacts and coaches, call the local sales office or sales manager, tell them what you are trying to do and request a research meeting. If you get one of these calls from a rep, help them out and give them a meeting!

Tip 68. What If?

What if the decision maker calls you? No, seriously! What if the decision maker calls you because she wants to do business with you? It happens, right? Not enough for any of us, but it does happen. Maybe one of your best customers left her company for a better opportunity. She appreciated your relationship and wants to capitalize on it again in her new setting. Once you're done pinching yourself, what do you do?

Here are a few ideas:

- Don't take anything for granted. Begin with a desire to do the same complete and compelling job selling to them that you did before.
- Start with your research, learning more about the new company, vision, opportunity and challenges.
- Set up a presentation meeting to discuss the potential fit and required actions.
- Ask who you need to do research with before this meeting in order to be best prepared.

This last point highlights an important subtlety about your research. Don't ask if you should do additional homework before your meeting. Instead, tell them you want to be best prepared for your meeting and ask them for the opportunity to do your research. Your request might sound something like this:

> *"I'm looking forward to our meeting on the 14th. I want to make sure I am prepared and can make the best use of your time. Who on your team do I need to do some research with in order to be best prepared?"*

No doubt this is tough. You work hard and get so few bluebirds. It's easy to immediately start calculating the revenues (and the commissions!) but don't fall into the trap. Work as hard for this sale as any other and justify their faith in you all over again.

Tip 69. A Huge Asset

One of the best ways to get a meeting with a decision maker is by leveraging our coach network. This is a great combination: high odds of success with little time investment.

Nonetheless, there are a couple of key variables to consider. First, we need to select the right coach to make this request. What makes someone the right coach? First, they need to be credible with the decision maker and therefore likely to be successful. This is where it really comes in handy to have a network of coaches, rather than a single coach. Second, they need to be comfortable making the request for a meeting.

In this regard, we shouldn't assume they know what needs to be said. Instead, we should take some time to coach them on the request. Talk it through with them and tell them what you would say if you were picking up the phone. Be sure to focus on getting an hour on the calendar to review a business presentation aimed at assisting them in accomplishing critical objectives and/or in addressing crucial issues. Focus on the most compelling objectives or issues based on your research and coach's input. Talk it through until you feel your coach is comfortable and confident. This will be a good use of a few minutes.

Coaches will go into this effort with good intentions, but good intentions don't pay the bills. Take a couple of minutes to coach your coach and increase your odds of successfully scheduling your presentation.

Tip 70. Like Rank Selling

In previous Tips, we talked about the strategy of using your team to help overcome some procurement-driven challenges. Tip #65 "Leveraging Your Assets" reviewed the strategy of utilizing various members of the team to reach out and do research with their contacts. Tip #34 "Use Your Team" presented the idea of leveraging your procurement team to help develop and execute a successful strategy.

Now we want to revisit a time-tested strategy: using your senior executives to reach out above Procurement to their senior executive counterparts in the customer organization. This can be effective for a number of reasons, including:

- They have every right to assess how their own organization is spending their resources.
- They have the ability to bring in the right resources based on the situation and may need to qualify the situation for themselves.
- They may not be bound by the same procurement rules.
- They don't have to face the gatekeeper or procurement contact on a daily basis.
- They have the ability to make decisions and concessions if the opportunity merits.
- They can take advantage of the professional courtesy that exists between many senior executives.

The beauty of this strategy is twofold. First, it's very effective. Second, we are not to blame for going around Procurement and the procurement process. It's not our fault that our executives feel the way they do, and we certainly cannot control their actions.

If we are going to use this strategy, we need to consider how to prepare our executives. If we assume they know what to say, we put them at a big disadvantage and set them up to fail. Instead, we can prepare a brief overview of the situation and the request we want them to make:

What is the opportunity?

What are the customer's objectives, strategies and issues?

Who is the executive we are calling, and what is the specific request we are making?

What are some of the elements of the fit that they can use to compel the executive?

By preparing this brief overview, we improve our odds of getting this key meeting scheduled.

Tip 71. Line 'em Up

An effective sales strategy to consider, especially in a significant sale where you are willing to invest your time and resources, is to align and leverage your team throughout the sales process. There are several people you may want to utilize:

Executive leadership team – Can you get one of the senior executives to commit to being an "executive sponsor" early on in this opportunity? By doing so, you can establish a tone of importance and priority with the customer, as your executive reaches out to their executives. In addition to building key relationships, this can also prevent us from getting blocked by a gatekeeper.

Pre-sales/solution design/technical salespeople – Knowledgeable solution experts play a key role on many sales teams and have a different type of credibility with customers. They are seen as more impartial and customer-focused. Leverage them for your research at a solution level and to build coach relationships at a user level.

Your manager – Your direct manager can help connect with your primary contact's managers, showing your company's commitment and ability to assign resources as needed.

Procurement – Your own procurement people can play a valuable role in your sales process, giving you guidance and reaching out to do research and build coach relationships with their counterparts.

Functional team players – If your solution involves a functional element like HR, Legal or IT, you can leverage your functional people to connect with their counterparts.

Customers – Of course, leveraging your own customers to connect with a prospect as a reference is commonly done—and if done right can be incredibly powerful.

Don't forget your best resource: yourself. You are the one person on the team accountable to build a powerful coach network. Leveraging other members of your team can be a powerful way to do this.

Tip 72. An Arrow in the Quiver

You need to get to a senior-level decision maker, but the traditional strategies like leveraging a coach, making the request yourself or getting your executives involved don't seem right. Maybe you don't have the right coaches who are credible to the decision maker, or you don't have the confidence that a personal request will get the job done.

What else can you do? One option is to use an IMPAX Access Letter, which is a letter designed specifically to help gain access to decision makers. This letter is different than the traditional sales letter. It doesn't go on and on about us; instead, it puts the focus on the customer: both the individual and the company.

Check out this really poor attempt to use a letter to get a meeting with a senior executive. (This is NOT an example of an IMPAX Access Letter.)

From:
Sent: Thursday, March 14, 2013 11:41 AM
To:
Subject: Following your business

I have been following your company lately and wanted to showcase our capabilities within Demand Generation, Telemarketing, TeleSales, Prospect Uncovering (Contact Database Building), and Marketing Database Updating that we currently provide to leading companies like Calypso, Websense, Bloomberg, Dow Jones, Bloomberg, Interactive Data, et al globally.

Our services revolve exclusively around B2B/Enterprise Data to leading industry (Media & Publishing, Technology, HealthCare, Finance, et al). Our services are industry agnostic. I have been reading about your company offerings and believe that our services might help make a tangible difference and reduce the cost per sales/lead with significant cost savings.

Our clients utilize our services for enhancing the response rate and ROI of their Demand Generation and Telemarketing campaigns. We would like to discuss with you our range of services that could help you control cost in the areas of marketing and connecting with your prospects to increase your leads pipeline and customer base.

"Let's set up a time to talk about this. We just need a 15-minute conversation to get started." I hope it's alright. What would be the best time to reach you in the week of March 18?

Look forward to hearing from you.
Best Regards,

Of course, in order to write an effective access letter, you need to do your research. You have to understand the biggest issues and opportunities this person is addressing, and then position yourself as someone who can help. For more on developing this letter, pre-selling the letter to improve the odds of getting it to the decision maker and samples to draw from, see Chapter 8 of <u>Beyond Selling Value</u>.

Remember, this letter is selling a meeting, not a product or solution. Keep the information about you and your products to a minimum and focus on the customer. Request an hour of their time. As a result, they might ask, "Why wouldn't I meet with someone who understands my business this well?"

This is an example of a successful IMPAX Access Letter.

Name
Title
Company

Dear...,

We recognize and respect the integral role that you play in guiding the sophisticated issues of risk management that impact (your company's) businesses.

Particularly in light of the current business climate of overcapacity, shrinking markets, and possibly disinflation, you may be reviewing such basic, yet pivotal, issues as:

- How to best manage the risks associated with the complexity of asset management flow and transaction businesses
- Defining the concentration of risk by assets and industry
- Evaluating the impact of specific customers across your businesses
- Protecting your AAA rating, particularly as it relates to determining acceptable levels of delinquencies

We are prepared to address these issues and others. That is why we are contacting you directly to schedule a presentation meeting.

As a point of reference, (our company) is currently very involved in all of (your company's) businesses. As a result, we are prepared to present recommendations, for your consideration, that can impact all (your company's) businesses.

Our presentation will be concise and the content relevant. This initial meeting can be held to under one hour.

I'll contact your office in a few days with the hope that (your assistant) can confirm your availability for our presentation, preferably during the week of (date).

I look forward to meeting you.
Cordially,

Tip 73. Quid Pro Quo

Reciprocity is another option to consider when trying to gain access to senior level executives. If your business is a good customer (or potential customer) of the company you are trying to win, this could be a good way to get to the right people. As an example, what if you are trying to gain inroads into an automobile manufacturer, and you learn that your own company buys its fleet vehicles from that manufacturer? This could be a very strategic piece of information.

....

"My sales team was engaged in selling to a major automotive company, and we couldn't get access to the senior management team. Then I realized that we purchased 2,000+ fleet vehicles from them every year and our competitors purchased none. We leveraged this in a non-threatening way to get an audience. That's all we wanted: a fair shot. It would've been foolish to ignore this asset, but we had to play it right."

Anonymous

....

Of course, you have to execute carefully. You don't want to overstep or infer that they have to meet with you. That could be considered unethical in some circles. Instead, you are trying to leverage professional courtesy simply to gain an audience with the right people and the opportunity to be considered a supplier/partner.

Keep in mind that if your company is a customer of your target account, there are no doubt people in that company who have a vested interest in your business and may be eager to help you. This could be a major asset in which to leverage. Consider the sales team and sales leadership as prime research and network contacts. If they want to keep you as a customer, they will want to help you be successful. This is another form of reciprocity that can be very effective: two business development professionals sharing insights to help each other be successful.

One warning to consider: There is a chance that one of your competitors has an even bigger relationship with the company. Do your research and don't overstep!

Tip 74. Get Your Act Together

Making a personal request of the decision maker is another strategy for scheduling a presentation.

The good news: in a study by Sirius Decisions and Ball State University, they found 98% of senior level executives decide for themselves whom they will meet for sales calls.

If you have credibility with the decision maker and are confident in your ability to get a "Yes," that's terrific! You have high odds of getting your meeting scheduled with a small amount of effort.

If you don't have a relationship with this person, your odds are lower and your job is bigger. You have a short amount of time to make a strong enough impression that they should spend time with you. Prepare for this meeting by thinking through and even writing out your request. Capture the key points of your request: you have been doing your research and understand a few of their key hot buttons; you recognize the role they play in the organization; you sense there could be a powerful fit between your companies as it pertains to these hot buttons; and you are asking for an hour to make a business presentation to reflect on this fit.

Review this outline every time you pick up the phone to call them, so you are prepared when they answer. You don't want to get caught unprepared, stammering when you should be compelling.

IMPAX MAXIM

"Information is not power. Applying information is power."

Tip 75. The Elevator Pitch

People have told us since we started our sales careers that we need to have a good "elevator pitch." They've given us the scenario that says, "You are the only person on an elevator, and you are going to the 15th floor. Just as the doors close, another person jumps in. You quickly realize that it's the senior executive from a key prospect you have been hoping to meet, and they pressed the button for floor 16. You have 15 floors, so 'Ready, Set, Pitch!'"

Conventional wisdom says we need to have our story perfectly honed. We have to convey who we are, what we do and how we do it in such a way that we compel them to want to spend more time with us. We should talk about our products, market presence, customer base, competitive advantage, etc.

The problem with this scenario is that it's all about us, and most people just don't care. What do they care about? Themselves! So maybe the pitch should sound more like an IMPAX Access Letter (see Tip #72 "An Arrow in the Quiver").

"Hello Mr. Smith. My name is ... and I represent .... As I have been doing my homework about your company, I learned that you may be focused on increasing revenues and driving your EBIT up beyond 15% (objectives). To accomplish this, you seem to be redesigning your supply chain and doubling your investment in R&D (strategies) while addressing increasing raw material costs and inaccurate customer perceptions (issues). Is my homework on target?"

Is this compelling? It depends on how accurate your research is.

After this, you should share briefly who your company is and how you may be able to assist them. Ask for a meeting. Keep your request short and if your research is on target, your odds of getting a "Yes" should increase dramatically.

Tip 76. The Elevator Pitch, Part 2

In our last Tip, we talked about the "Elevator Pitch" and one of the challenges with it: it's typically all about us. Will this inspire the decision maker we've been fortunate enough to run into? It probably won't, even if we have our story perfectly honed. Our conclusion: maybe the Elevator Pitch should sound more like an IMPAX Access Letter. If we share briefly the key things we learned about the customer's business, they would most likely find this more interesting and be more likely to give us a meeting.

The problem with this alternative is that it requires us to have done our research. What if we haven't had a chance to do this? If we can't articulate the key elements of their business direction, we shouldn't take a risk by winging it.

So what should we do? After all, we have to take advantage of this opportunity. Instead of giving them an Elevator Pitch, why not ask an "Elevator Question?" It may sound something like this:

"Hello Mr. Smith. My name is ... and I represent .... I have been doing my homework on your company, and I would love to ask you a quick question. What's the biggest issue facing your company today?"

Other questions you could ask:

"How will your company be different two years from now?"

"I've heard about your aggressive growth targets. How will you accomplish these?"

"Could you share with me your vision for the company?"

Asking questions like these demonstrates your genuine interest in learning more about them and their business. Many executives will find this more inspiring and compelling than a generic pitch about our products and capabilities.

Keep in mind one last question: "Once I've completed my research, could I schedule a brief meeting with you to review what I've learned and to discuss the potential business fit between our companies?"

IMPAX MAXIM

"People would rather talk about themselves than listen to us talk about ourselves!"

Tip 77. Stand Up and Stand Out!

A sales leader recently said, "The problem with these RFPs is that it's impossible to differentiate ourselves through ink on paper. We just all blend together." It's true, and this is one of the key reasons that Procurement finds them effective. They "level the playing field" and drive focus on price instead of value.

If you want to stand out, what's the best way to deliver an RFP response? It's not by mailing or emailing it. It's by showing up in person, getting on your feet and delivering your response through a presentation! Why stand and present? Because:

- This is the best way to communicate your enthusiasm and passion.
- It is a powerful differentiation strategy.
- Many of your competitors don't do this.
- It will dramatically improve your odds of success!

Delivering your response via a presentation also gives you an opportunity to show how your solution meets their requirements and how your value-oriented relationship could drive real business results. You can give them all of the information they need on the proposal while bringing the business fit to life.

One concern some might have with this strategy is the amount of work associated with putting together and delivering a presentation. Realistically, it probably takes a lot less time than we think, and we have to ask, "If it's worth putting all the effort into creating an RFP response, is it worth putting in a little more effort to improve our odds of success?"

• •

"We know the value of standing up and presenting throughout the sales cycle, whether it's a solution overview, a proposal response, a business presentation about the fit between our companies or a closing meeting. When we get on our feet, everything changes – our energy level ramps up, we gain control of the meeting, our confidence grows, our passion comes through, and our clients, prospects and partners look at us differently. We love to compete against people who mail it in or just sit and discuss their RFP response."

Jeff Vint
Vice President, Specialty Markets
TCF Equipment Finance

• •

Tip 78. The Mirror Doesn't Lie

So you've got a big presentation and no one to rehearse with. Not only that, but you are in a hotel room and the presentation is tomorrow morning. What's a good way to rehearse? Use a mirror. Literally, set yourself up so you make the presentation in front of a mirror and are forced to watch yourself. This may not be a lot of fun and chances are it may be frustrating, but that doesn't mean it won't be effective. When you watch yourself present, you get to see what others see. Are you smiling? What are you doing with your hands? Do you know your stuff? Do you have any annoying mannerisms? Do you look comfortable?

Of course, videotaping your rehearsal session and reviewing it can be very helpful (and painful!) in assessing and improving the use of gestures, eye contact, use of media, body movements and verbal delivery. However, many of us can focus so much on the verbal delivery (pace, volume, choice of words, non-words) that we miss other key learnings. For additional insight, review the video with the sound off, which will lend an entirely new perspective. See what looks wrong and ask someone else for their feedback. Then fix it.

As with any rehearsal session, try to stay in role for a period of time and deal with mistakes in the same way you would in a real-world environment. Then learn from your mistakes and try it again. Focus first on getting the content down and then move on to improving your delivery. In the end, work hard enough that your confidence is high and you at least appear to be enjoying yourself. Your presentations will be more compelling, and your presence will be more inspiring.

Yes, these rehearsal sessions can be potentially awkward and uncomfortable, but so is making a presentation without the right amount of rehearsal!

Tip 79. Rehearsal What-Ifs

There are many steps to prepare for different activities in the sales cycle. One powerful strategy is to utilize the "what-if" question, which allows us to test our readiness for a given activity.

As an example, consider this situation: you are rehearsing for an upcoming presentation. As you hone your mastery of the content and refine your delivery, you begin to ask yourself some "what-if" questions.

Examples of questions you might consider in this context include:

What if the decision maker doesn't show up for the presentation meeting?

What if the decision maker is late?

What if the decision maker is late and the rest of the group wants to get started before he arrives?

What if a gatekeeper tries to take me off track with technical questions?

What if something goes wrong with my presentation medium?

What if the decision maker tells me I have less time than expected?

What if my manager, who is attending the presentation, doesn't understand what I am trying to accomplish?

What if the decision maker doesn't like my suggested action steps?

What if the decision maker agrees with my suggested action steps and wants to move forward?

These types of questions are very helpful in your preparation activities. They'll help you be prepared for things that can go wrong—and help you be ready when things go right!

> *"Practice isn't the thing you do once you're good. It's the thing you do that makes you good."*
>
> Malcolm Gladwell

Tip 80. Likeability

What is "likeability," and why are we talking about it? Well, when it comes to making effective and compelling presentations, likeability is an important attribute. This is even more important as you deal with Procurement and departmental executives. You don't want to appear adversarial or standoffish.

This makes sense, but can you build or develop likeability, or do you just have it (or not)? Let's hope for the sake of those of us who aren't immediately likeable that you can indeed embody it!

How do you portray likeability? First, you can smile. This may seem too simple to mention, but we've all seen presenters who didn't smile. As a result, they didn't seem happy or excited to be at the meeting. If the presenter isn't happy or excited, how will the audience feel? What if the presenter had a tough morning, was up late with the kids, experienced car trouble, spilled coffee on themselves, etc.? What if it's obvious to the audience that the presenter had a tough morning?

A second way to be more likeable is to use everyone's favorite word: their name. It's a compliment to audience members that you remember and use their names. Get their business cards, write up a seating chart, do whatever you need to be able to use their names—but be careful. You don't want to overdo it. When you use their names too often, it can sound contrived or insincere.

A third way to appear likeable is to have a high-energy level. It should look to the audience like you are excited to be there.

Lastly, remember that this is supposed to be fun! The reason many of us got into business development is because we love to spend time with customers and prospects, and presentations are a chance for us to shine. Enjoy them!

Tip 81. Turning a Negative into a Positive

We've responded to the RFP, and we made the cut! Now we're a finalist. We get to come in for "vendor day" and make our final presentation along with the other three finalists. All of the finalists must present to the same decision team on the same day. In fact, we are told what our presentation should look like and what format to follow.

Vendor day can sometimes be a drag. We're told what to do, how to do it and when to do it. All of our creativity and innovation are negated, and we can end up feeling like trained dogs jumping through hoops. Now, of course, there's good news, too. We made the cut and should be happy. But the bad news is that we are in a head-to-head competition where the focus is on our solution and our pricing. But what if our solutions are pretty similar and our pricing is a little higher? What if our true value doesn't show up on a vendor grid?

If that's the case, the first thing we need to do is look at the situation differently than our competition. They may be looking at this as an opportunity to show off their products and propose their pricing. We need to look at this as an opportunity to highlight a compelling business and solution fit between the companies. As a result, we need to conduct a different type of research so that we walk into the meeting understanding the customer's solution needs and business direction.

What a great opportunity to truly differentiate ourselves from the competition! We just have to change the basis of comparison and our presentation. We don't want to look just like everybody else. We can still give the customer the information they requested, but do it in a way that highlights the unique value and the strength of the business fit between our companies. We can differentiate ourselves not just on what we are selling and how much we are selling it for, but on how we do business.

Tip 83. Presenting to a Committee

The comedian Milton Berle once said, "Committees are groups that keep minutes and lose hours." We can all appreciate that quote. The only thing worse than selling to a committee is being on one!

Many sales cycles or RFPs have a rule that calls for a presentation to a committee that "supposedly" makes the decision. "Supposedly" because committees rarely make decisions; they make recommendations. More to the point, they seem to make decisions as long as it's the one the real decision maker wants.

Before blindly agreeing to make our presentation, here are a few questions to ask (ourselves and our coaches):

Who sits on the committee?

What roles do the participants play?

Who leads the committee?

If the committee were a jury, who would be the foreman?

What coalitions and rivalries exist?

Do we have a coach or coaches on the committee?

Who are we aligned with, and how influential are they?

What relationships do our competitors have with committee members?

Who put the committee in place?

How visible is this group?

What are their objectives, strategies and concerns?

What is the charter of the committee?

What is the track record of the committee?

Is it a standing committee or a one-time effort?

Will the decision maker attend our presentation?

Once we know the answers or can at least make educated guesses, we are in a much better position to decide if presenting to the committee is in our best interest and a good use of our time.

Tip 84. The Site Visit

So you got your prospect to come for a site visit or a visit to your headquarters. That's great! Now you have to make the most of the opportunity. Having a successful site visit often means making sure the customer hears the right messages, meets the right people, sees the operation and has a chance to ask their top-of-mind questions.

Here's another thing you can do: kick-off the meeting with a high-impact business presentation. This is effective for a number of reasons. First, you start the day by focusing on the customer, which sets a positive tone. Second, you can clarify everyone's expectations for the day. This is an ideal time to ask the questions, "What do you want to see today?" or "What would make this a great day?"

This presentation also gives the day a focal point. You can kick-off the day with the presentation, highlight the business fit, have your roundtable discussion where the key action step is to go out and conduct your site visit, and then come back to the conference room and review the business fit and additional action steps after the tour. This gives you a chance to close the meeting effectively, laying out the optimal plan to keep the process moving.

These same ideas apply to an important demo. Why not follow the "Them, Us, Fit and Action" flow to make the most of your demo opportunity?

Tip 85. You Make the Call

Here's a tough situation that can arise before or during a key sales or relationship management presentation: The decision maker tells you she no longer has an hour (or whatever you had originally scheduled) and only has a few minutes. Once we've clarified exactly how much time she has for the meeting, we have a call to make. Can we make an effective presentation in that time, or should we try to reschedule?

Unfortunately, there is no easy answer to this question, and this is a time when your experience (the art of sales) can really come in handy. Questions going through your mind might include:

Why has this happened? Is it a legitimate issue, or does she not see the value in our meeting?

Can I edit my presentation down to a timeframe that works?

Can I be compelling enough in the time available?

What is the minimum amount of time I need to be compelling?

Will I be able to easily reschedule?

Will this postponement/rescheduling effort become a cancellation?

How difficult or expensive was it to get here?

How difficult or expensive will it be to get back for our next meeting?

What are the odds that next time the situation will be more favorable?

In other words, will you lose the opportunity if you don't plow ahead, and can you make a strong enough impression in the time you have?

Clearly there is no easy answer. It really does depend on the answers to the questions above. If you believe you can easily and quickly reschedule, you may want to do it. If you believe you have no chance once you leave, go for it. By the way, you won't get much time to think about these questions when you are "live." It's best to think about them during your rehearsal sessions.

One last thought: If you are following the IMPAX presentation format of "Them, Us, Fit, Action," you will be starting your presentation with a focus on the customer's business. This may make such a strong impression that you get more time than you expected.

Tip 86. Maintaining Control

Handling attendee questions is one of the toughest challenges we can encounter when delivering an IMPAX presentation. Questions in this context can be a concern because we want to maintain control of the presentation, ensuring that we complete the formal aspect of the presentation and transition into a roundtable discussion in a timely way. We want interaction during our meeting, just not while we're delivering the presentation.

Here are some thoughts about handling questions during a presentation:

Assess the question – Is it well intended? Is it a sincere question or one designed to trip us up? Does answering this particular question enhance our efforts?

Consider the source – If the question comes from a decision maker, a brief answer is in order. If it comes from a gatekeeper, it could be a trap. Even if the question is well intended, it could require a degree of technical depth that the decision maker doesn't need. Going too deep with your answer can cause you to lose the decision maker's attention.

Defer the answer – A comfortable way to address this issue is to defer the answer to the roundtable discussion by saying something like, "Thank you for the question. Let's address this in a couple of minutes during our roundtable discussion."

Make a note – You can show your interest in the question by writing it down on a whiteboard, a flipchart or in your notebook, so you will remember to come back to it.

Answer quickly – If you decide to answer the question, clarify it and answer it, getting back into your presentation flow quickly.

Maintaining control of the presentation is critical to driving the desired outcome. You've done your research and now is the time to shine through your presentation. Skillfully and sensitively deferring questions will help to maximize the outcome of both the presentation and the roundtable discussion.

Tip 87. Go Out With a Bang

Earlier in this section, we talked about making the most of the presentation by rehearsing effectively. One of the benefits of good rehearsal is that it can help us to get off to a strong start and nail the opening. The first 90 seconds set the tone for the rest of the meeting and if we get the opening right our confidence will soar.

Let's build on that theme by talking about the other place in the presentation where a little extra rehearsal goes a long way: the closing. After all, we don't make IMPAX presentations so we can say we made a great executive presentation. We make them so we can close on our desired action.

Many times, we've seen a terrific, well-delivered presentation end with a whimper instead of a bang. What a disappointment. Delivering a powerful presentation is a great set up for a strong close, and a great way to accomplish this is to plan for it and rehearse it.

The first step in writing an IMPAX presentation is to write the last page: the "Action Steps" page. We do this so the desired outcome is top of mind for us as we write the rest of it. In doing this, we put the close first, building every page around it. After all, in most presentations, the roundtable discussion that follows the formal presentation is driven by what's on the Action Steps page.

A key step in this process is to determine your closing question. Consider the decision maker's style, the coaches and gatekeepers in attendance and the nature of your request. Then come up with very specific questions as you transition to the roundtable discussion. Some examples:

"These are my recommendations. How do you feel we should proceed?"

"Should we move ahead on these action steps at this time?"

"Is there anything that stands between us and moving forward on these recommendations?"

Any of these may work fine—given your situation—and there are many other ways you can ask your question. The two keys are that you ask a pointed, direct question, and that you leverage the answer to direct your roundtable discussion, determining commitments, timeframes and responsibilities.

Whatever you do, rehearse your close several times, so your great closing question doesn't turn into, "So, what do you think?" or "Any thoughts about what we should do now?" Practice delivering your Recommendations or Action Steps page, while literally transitioning from presenting at the front of the room to sitting down and joining the roundtable discussion, all the while looking the decision maker in the eyes. This will show the group that the roundtable is as important as the rest of the presentation, and that you are ready to guide them to a meaningful conclusion.

Tip 88. The Closing Question

Closing (effectively) is one of the most difficult yet satisfying steps in the sales process. When done right, closing is a natural element that leaves all parties feeling successful. When it's done wrong, it can derail an otherwise "done deal." Closing strategies like the Puppy Dog, the Expiring Offer and the Bait and Switch can come across as tricky, sleazy or worse.

When done well, the closing process is so natural: You review what the prospect is trying to accomplish, position your ability to be a resource, present the business and solution fit and make your recommendations on how to proceed. Then you ask THE question:

"These are my recommendations. How do you feel we should proceed?"

The beauty of this question is that it directs the answer back to your recommendations. When this question is asked, the subject has three basic options:

- They can react to your recommendations, opening the door to a fruitful discussion (the most common outcome);
- They can say they have other ideas about how to move forward (a rare but very productive outcome); or
- They can tell you they don't want to proceed (a less common outcome that leads to a whole new set of questions and opportunities).

This question needs to be asked. It's a natural part of the process that doesn't feel contrived in any way. After all, it's our job to get the customer to the point where they are excited and ready to take the next step.

••

"Closing is a funny thing. It's very logical but can still be really hard to execute. Done well, it sets the tone for a win-win path forward. Done poorly, it can cause irreparable harm. One of our reps showed the way when he asked a CEO one of the simplest closing questions I have ever heard, "Based on what we have discussed today Tamara, how do you think I should proceed?" She looked at him and simply said, "I think you should send me a contract with the pricing in it". We weren't necessarily expecting this response, so when we recovered we did exactly that, and we were off to the races. Now we try to emulate this in all of our sales opportunities. We make sure to close the right person, and we keep the question simple, direct and professional. It works well for us!"

Jeff Chester
Chief Revenue Officer and SVP
Availity

••

Tip 89. What's the Cost?

There is a great closing question you can ask, which is a tough one for a customer to answer. It can sound like a trap, but it isn't meant to be. It can be used in either a research or presentation setting. What's the question? "What does it cost you not to make this decision?" or closely-related versions:

"What does it cost you not to move forward and begin implementation now?" (putting the focus on implementation);

"What does it cost you in lost opportunities if you delay?" (maybe there are some milestones that won't get reached or some windows of opportunity that might close);

"What obstacles can crop up if this decision isn't made soon?" (this can get them to think about "striking while the iron is hot" or spending the money in the budget before it gets taken away); or

"What are some cost and budget items that might be affected if this decision doesn't get made soon?" (variable costs, like energy rates and currency exchange rates are known now but uncertain in the near future).

This is a great question if you are in a research setting with a knowledgeable coach; in a non-competitive setting where the decision maker is on the fence, hesitating and wondering if the time is right; or if you are at a minor price difference as compared to a competitor, and you can compensate by showing how you can drive more immediate implementation and realize the benefits sooner.

The intent of this question is to get the customer thinking about the flip side of a buying decision. It's easy and natural to think about what a decision costs but not quite as easy to think about what it costs NOT to make a decision.

If you are going to use this type of question, it's important to be sincere, or at least seem like you are!

"The key to success in life is sincerity and as soon as you can fake that you've got it made."

Jean Giraudoux, playwright

Tip 90. The Price Question

> A passerby knocked at the door of a farmhouse and asked the farmer, "How much is that old bull out there on the road worth to you?" The farmer replied, "That depends—are you the tax assessor, do you want to buy him, or did you run him down with your truck?"

One of the toughest questions in a buying cycle or RFP is the pricing question. Why so tough? Sometimes:

- The request is so vague we don't know what to give them.
- The request is so early we don't even have a specific solution in mind yet.
- The request is so broad that it's mind boggling to figure out what price to give them.
- Our pricing is in flux based on supply, demand, market considerations and timing, and we truly don't know what our price will be at an undefined date.
- We aren't sure what the negotiation process will be.
- We don't know how important the pricing criteria are at this stage and whether our response, or lack thereof, might eliminate us from consideration or position us as a front runner.

We can often end up feeling like we have to give them our best shot at the RFP response stage just to become a finalist, fully realizing that if we get to this stage, we'll be asked to go lower, all before entering the true negotiation phase!

One of our clients is typically asked to provide market basket pricing, meaning pricing for every single item they offer down to the smallest one, whether or not those items are even part of the solution. The workload associated with gathering and providing this information is intimidating.

There is certainly no easy solution to this problem, but we do have options. We can give them what they ask for; give them a sampling of our pricing; share with them our pricing philosophy and typical market positioning; or defer specific pricing until the solution is clearer. The intent is not to avoid the topic but to make sure that when we address it, we address it effectively and avoid an endless discounting loop.

In any case, we need to make sure that our answer to their price question reflects the value we bring.

Several years ago, NFL Hall of Fame Quarterback Fran Tarkenton, who has followed up his playing career with a successful broadcasting, business and speaking career, was asked to give a speech for half of his typical fee. His response was immediate:

"Of course I can. Which half of the speech would you like? The front half or back half?"

Fran Tarkenton

Tip 91. References Required

In many buying cycles, prospects request or even demand references as a key part of our response. These references typically include the names of companies as well as the names of specific people who can testify to our abilities.

These references are part of our unique value. They are assets, and it takes effort to leverage them. We have to determine the right references for each situation, get to the people on our team who "own" these relationships, contact the individual and position our request. We also have to worry about going to the well too often.

This process can be frustrating to our references, as well. We reach out to them, position our request, they agree to help and in many cases, no one ever calls them. The reason: The situation was never qualified in the first place. We needed to provide the references as a condition of our response but since we never became a finalist, no one ever reached out to them.

Needless to say, our references are assets, and we only want to use them in qualified situations. When responding to an opportunity, we don't have to follow the exact rules. One option is to provide the company names of appropriate customers and mention that specific contact names will be provided at the right time. Or you can go further and say that specific contact names will be provided just prior to or just following your business presentation to the decision maker or decision team. The more we recognize the value of our references, the more likely our prospects will, as well.

One last idea: One compelling way to use a reference is to have him or her call your prospect. This takes a unique and powerful coach relationship, but this can have a unique and powerful impact.

Tip 92. Mutual Agreement

One of the ironies we encounter when responding to RFPs is that we are constantly asked to sign non-disclosure agreements (NDAs) while at the same time not often given an opportunity to protect our own intellectual property and pricing information. Why is this? Probably because this is what the customer is demanding, and they have all of the power. It's disheartening to think that our souls are laid bare for everyone to see. Some prospects and customers have gone so far as to put our RFP responses on the Internet: pricing and all. To say the least, this can be terribly damaging to our competitive positioning.

Maybe it's time to take some of that power back by asking for a mutual NDA instead of a traditional NDA. In exchange for our confidentiality with regards to their sensitive information, we ask for the same treatment of our confidential information about our services, future direction, delivery strategies, pricing, terms, etc. All we want is the same respect for our confidential information that the prospect is asking from us.

On the surface, this should be an easy one. How could someone argue this is unfair to the prospect? If it is good for them, it should be good for us, too. Maybe in reality, this won't sit so well with them. If that is the case, this might be the perfect time to ask more about their process and what they plan to do with the information we provide them. Maybe we need to ask the question up front: "What is your plan for handling our confidential information?" Their answer is important, and we need to factor this in as we think about the format of our response, the depth of what we share and our overall interest in working with this customer.

Tip 93. Move Cautiously

In many buying cycles, there is a request for references (see Tip #91 "References Required" for thoughts on providing references). Another version of this is the request for an overview of your relevant industry experience. This can be a loaded question!

Why? Well, we have a few questions to ask before we provide our response:

Who are we competing against, and how does our industry experience compare to that of our competition?

How does our prospect view their competitors? Which of those do they respect and which ones do they not respect? How do they feel about those we've worked with?

How important is our ability to help the customer create or strengthen their competitive advantage?

How strongly does the decision maker feel about this topic?

There is a chance this is a deal breaker either way, and we need to know before we answer. How does the decision maker feel about their competitor? Does he think his competition is well run and that he would like to work with the companies that have helped his competition get ahead? Or does he want to stay ahead of them and continue to out-innovate them—and not use the same resources? Or that he needs to leap-frog the competition with some unique capabilities? Might he have some concerns about confidentiality or intellectual property that he may not want to trust to a vendor who is close to his competition?

Date
Name
Title
Company

Hello,

My name is (name) and I am a sales representative for (company). We recently supported a client whose products and markets are very similar to yours. I am sharing an LED sign solution that helps your product stand out. I have enclosed a brief deck sharing the idea along with a portable digital messaging tool solution.

(Our company) is a leading visual brand company. We make brands shine. We have a creative and manufacturing emphasis in the development of high quality LED signs and merchandising and display solutions. We have the reputation for pioneering technological innovation to improve performance of our products and reduce costs.

I visit your city every four to six weeks. I will follow up with you to determine if we can set up a meeting to discuss the shared solutions and review a LED sample we created for one of your competitors.

Sincerely,

This letter was sent to a client of ours. The sales rep featured work they had just completed with our client's biggest competitor, whom they despised. This strategy completely backfired! There has to be a better way …

As always, research is critical to help us create the best strategy. We don't just have to answer their questions. We have to fashion our response in a way that gives us an advantage. The answers to these questions can help us determine if we want to tout or underplay our vast industry experience, or cover up or capitalize on our lack of experience with their competitors.

Tip 94. Competitive Position

Everyone in business development has to face competitive pressures, and we need to choose our strategy carefully. Unfortunately, many of us don't.

The most common competitive strategies we use include:

Head to head – where we compete on an even playing field against a competitor.

Change the ground rules – where we try to change the basis of comparison to our favor.

Divide and conquer – where we try to win a small piece of the business in the short-term to help us win a bigger opportunity down the road.

Delay – we use this when we are in a weak position and need to buy some time until conditions change.

In addition, many also consider **"setting traps"** as a viable strategy. Using this strategy, we (or our coaches) place traps for our competitors to strengthen our own position.

All of these strategies have a time and a place where they can be effective, yet most people rely almost solely on the first option: competing on a head-to-head basis. On the surface, this makes sense, as this is what the customer's buying process is trying to get us to do. However, there are times when this is not a good strategy (e.g. maybe we are the value leader and the client is emphasizing low price). Some believe that in order to use this approach, we should have a clear two-to-one advantage over our competitor. That sets the bar pretty high!

This is another area where breaking the rules, or changing the ground rules, can have a big impact. There are a number of ways we can do this, including:

- Getting to senior-level decision makers;
- Involving our own senior-level executives;
- Moving from an apples-to-apples comparison to an apples-to-oranges comparison;
- Positioning the solution fit and business fit we bring to the table; and
- Submitting multiple responses to an opportunity—one that meets their specs and one that more significantly impacts their business.

Changing the rules can involve risks, but it can also have big rewards.

Tip 95. Populate the Field

Many of us face a difficult reality: We have to sell to both a specific department (e.g. IT, Marketing, Supply Chain, etc.) and Procurement. We all know how difficult it can be just to win the support of the key players in a sales opportunity. We have to build coach relationships, deal effectively with evaluators/gatekeepers and compel decision makers.

For many, that is now the first hurdle. Next, we have to deal with Procurement, whose power varies from organization to organization. In some companies, Procurement may simply play the role of chief negotiator. In other companies, it may actually have the power to override the decision made by the department (happily, this is still quite rare).

Bringing these two strategies together at specific points in the sales process is one strategy to consider:

> **The research phase** – If you can effectively include Procurement in the research process, you may find yourself ahead of the game later. This could make Procurement feel involved and valued from the beginning, and you could gain critical insights. This could be dangerous if Procurement has the power to play the role of gatekeeper and restrict your access or strategy.

> **The presentations** – Imagine a meeting where you are making a powerful presentation and Procurement is one of the attendees. You have the opportunity to compel the decision maker, leverage the open support of your coaches and show Procurement how powerful your business and solution fit can be.

One of our clients used this strategy recently when they delivered a business presentation and proposal to an audience including both the department and Procurement. The Director of Procurement said, **"This was the first time my team has recommended a supplier where pricing wasn't the key decision-making factor."** He went on to commend the entire account team on a **"fantastic job accomplishing what your competitors could not, developing a creative and strategic proposal demonstrating why our joint relationship represents the best value."**

• •

"We really work hard to sell the value associated with our solutions and we knew we weren't going to win by having the lowest price. We thought we could get the support of the line executive, but weren't sure how the procurement leader would feel, so we were thrilled to hear his reaction after our presentation. Getting them both together turned out to be a great strategy. It appeared thorough and inclusive, didn't offend the procurement leader, we got credit for our value and it shortened the sales cycle."

Anne McKeough
Vice President of Global Sales
Staples Promotional Products

• •

Real World Application

Consider this situation faced by an IMPAX client:

Our client was a large retirement services provider who was pursuing a new account opportunity at a large retailer.

The procurement department of the retailer was working with an outside consulting company to help them evaluate several suppliers.

They were asked to come in and make a finalist's presentation.

They were given one hour and a very specific agenda to follow right down to the minute.

What would you do?

What did they do?

They determined that following the requested flow would completely commoditize them and not allow their company to differentiate themselves and position them to win on the value they brought to the table. So, they changed the ground rules and used an IMPAX RFP Finalist Presentation format (see Appendix E for a sample). They did address everything Procurement asked for but did it within the IMPAX "TUFA" format.

At the start of the presentation, they said, "we know there are certain things we need to address but we are going to take a few minutes to present what we think is a strong business fit between our two organizations", and that is what they did.

They received incredible feedback right away from the participants. As a matter of fact, the top executive from the prospect called the senior executive from our client and thanked him for his team coming in and told him how impressed he was with how much they understood their business. On top of that, the consulting company's key contact (who typically would stay neutral) told our client that what they did in that presentation really made the difference. They went on to win the business!

Tip 96. Populate the Field, Part II

In our last Tip, we talked about a challenge many of us are facing: the requirement to sell both to the procurement organization and the specific department that needs our solution. We shared a couple of times when it's good to bring the two groups together: the research phase and the presentation phase.

What is the value of bringing these two groups together?

- To involve Procurement and show they are a respected player in the process and
- To expose Procurement to your business and solution fit and to the reactions of your coaches and decision makers.

Another reason to do this is to get your coaches and decision makers to exert their influence on Procurement, helping to get you through the procurement stage intact.

Given this motivation, here is another time to bring these interested parties together: the negotiation phase. Often, the process is fairly sequential. After we get the endorsement of the buying department, we move to the negotiation stage with Procurement. After working hard to prove the fit, we now have to negotiate with Procurement, who is trained to disregard the value of the fit. This can be frustrating at best and a deal breaker at worst.

To minimize the pain, try bringing your decision maker or influential coach into the negotiation process. If they see you are being treated unreasonably, they might step in and support your position. Even if they won't do it in front of you, they might do it behind the scenes. This can be a viable strategy because at this stage, the decision maker has decided he needs and wants to work with you. The last thing he wants is for you to be chased from the account by an overly aggressive procurement person.

Tip 97. Populate the Field, Part III

In our last two Tips, we talked about the value associated with bringing two different groups together during the sales cycle: your buying department and the procurement organization. Here is another opportunity to bring them together: the relationship review presentation.

In a relationship review presentation, you are periodically presenting to the customer a formal review of the relationship, which can include the following topics:

- An update on your understanding of the customer's business direction (from your ongoing research efforts);
- An update on your company;
- A review of the relationship between the two companies: the activities you've been conducting, the successes you've experienced, the challenges you've encountered (and how you resolved them) and the value created by your joint efforts;
- The business fit; and
- Your recommendations and suggested action steps.

These presentations are typically delivered to the departmental executives you work with and can be very powerful. The best of these presentations go the deepest on the value assessment topic. The more you can quantify the value and the business fit, the more compelling your presentation becomes.

By inviting the appropriate people from Procurement to these presentations, they can better understand:

- The value you bring to their organization;
- The strength of your relationship with their counterparts (who, of course, are their customers);
- Your commitment to their success; and
- The proactive approach you have to managing the relationship.

These presentations can help you move from vendor to strategic resource. Will they completely negate the efforts of the procurement department to drive your prices down? Probably not, but if they help take the heat off a little, then they are worth it!

See Appendix F for a sample IMPAX Business Relationship Review Presentation.

Tip 98. The Last Resort

What if you've tried almost everything to deal with a tough procurement situation and are still blocked? Here's a "last resort" idea: change your team. It might sound extreme but by changing your team, you may be able to change the odds in your favor.

Your team—including sales reps, account managers, support and service personnel and front line managers—is the daily face of your company to the customer. They have their roles and relationships, and the customer can become accustomed to these people. They can also get blocked and trapped into playing by certain rules.

By replacing any of these people, you have a chance to stir things up. New players can leverage their "ignorance" and contact people the existing team might not be able to contact. They can skirt around gatekeepers because they simply "don't know any better." They can ask questions the current players might not be comfortable asking, such as, "Who will sign off on this project?" or "When will we meet with the decision team?" This all makes perfect sense, as the new players feel they need to do their homework and meet as many people as possible in order to understand and serve the customer better.

Replacing an executive sponsor can also be effective. New executive sponsors have a need to reach out and meet their counterparts, which are often the senior-level decision makers we need to gain access to for critical presentations and decisions. It is common and expected that these connections happen for all of the right reasons.

This is not a strategy you can take lightly or overuse but by making these changes, your team may be able to circumvent established processes and relationships and improve your odds of winning.

Tip 99. Pumped Up

We need to prepare to execute our procurement and sales strategy by getting our head on straight and getting fired up! Remember what we are doing and why we are doing it:

- We are business professionals, not vendors.
- We are highly trained and bring a depth of knowledge, experience and creativity to our customers and prospects.
- We specialize in helping our customers improve the way they do business.
- The more successful we are, the more successful our customers will be.

These reasons alone should make us excited about executing our plan. Ralph Waldo Emerson once said, "Nothing great was ever accomplished without enthusiasm." That makes sense, and we are going to need enthusiasm if we are to accomplish something great, such as overcoming a procurement gatekeeper to win an opportunity we were supposed to lose. In addition, enthusiasm is infectious, and if you "infect" your entire team with enthusiasm and positive energy, there is no telling what could happen.

Something else to keep in mind: It is more difficult to block a positive and enthusiastic professional than an insecure person who keeps looking over his shoulder in fear. There may be a lot of people who want to keep us down and commoditize us but if we do the right things, we can be the exception to the rule—and that's exciting!

Tip 100. Glass Half Full

A guy from Detroit dies and is sent to Hell. He had been a horrible man his entire life. The devil puts him to work breaking up rocks with a sledgehammer. To make it worse, he cranks up the temperature and the humidity.

After a couple of days, the devil checks in on his victim to see if he is suffering adequately. The devil is aghast as the Detroit native is happily swinging his hammer and whistling a happy tune.

The devil walks up to him and says, "I don't understand this. I've turned the heat way up, it's humid, and you're crushing rocks...Why are you so happy?"

With a big smile, he looks at the devil and replies, "This is great it reminds me of August in Detroit – hot, humid, a good place to work. It reminds me of home. This is fantastic!"

The devil, extremely perplexed, walks away to ponder the man's remarks. Then he decides to drop the temperature, send down a driving rain and torrential wind. Soon Hell is a wet, muddy mess.

Walking in mud up to his knees with dust blowing into his eyes, the man is happily slogging thru the mud pushing a wheelbarrow full of crushed rocks.

Again, the devil asks how he can be happy in such conditions. The man replies, "This is great! Just like April in Detroit. It reminds me of working out in the yard and spring planting!"

The devil is now completely baffled but more determined to make the man suffer. He makes the temperature plummet. Suddenly Hell is blanketed in snow and ice. Confident that this will surely make the man unhappy, the devil checks on him. He is again aghast at what he sees. The man is dancing, singing, and twirling his sledgehammer as he cavorts in glee.

"How can you be so happy? Don't you know it's 60 below zero?!" screams the devil.

Jumping up and down, the man throws a snowball at the devil and yells, "Hell's frozen over!! This means the Lions won the Super Bowl!"

We could easily cite countless studies that demonstrate that being optimistic is a more compelling trait for salespeople than being pessimistic, or that optimistic salespeople are more successful than pessimistic salespeople. Instead, let's just logically think through this. If you were a customer, who would you rather work with: a person with a positive outlook or a person with a gloomy outlook?

Does that mean it's always easy to maintain a rosy outlook? Of course not. It really is tough out there. Demanding customers, desperate competitors and challenging economic conditions, not to mention the constant pressure to perform, can weigh us down and dampen our outlook.

Nonetheless, there are salespeople who really believe it when they say "I don't mind a 'no' because I know that just brings me closer to a 'yes!'" These are the real "glass half full" people.

Can we train ourselves to be positive? Absolutely! It's like anything else we do in sales. We can become more effective if we think about it and work on it. Take a minute and count your blessings. Heck, if you are in sales and are reading this, you have at least a couple of them right there! Now do this exercise every day, and you can start to train yourself to be more positive.

The reality is that everyone experiences setbacks. The pessimist comes to expect them and accept them, creating his own reality. The optimist is convinced that tough times don't last forever, and she can learn something from these challenges. As a result, positive salespeople are less likely to take a loss personally. Maybe that's why optimism is an increasingly attractive trait in sales candidates!

"Tough times don't last, but tough people do!"
Robert H. Schuller

Tip 101. Get Input

We are surrounded by valuable assets to leverage in our business development efforts. These assets are the people we work with, and they can be invaluable to our success. In many cases, they are our coaches, too. As we know, coaches don't just reside in the customer's organization. Our coach network includes anyone who wants us to win and wins when we win.

As you develop your strategy, it's always helpful to get other perspectives from:

- Your support team (implementation, operations, IT, HR, finance, legal, etc.), who may have great perspectives on what it will take to make things work after the sale;
- Your fellow salespeople, who have "been there, done that" and may have experience from which you can benefit;
- Members of your leadership team, who have an executive perspective and keen insights (and whose support we need);
- Your mentors, who always seem to know what's about to happen just before it happens (no matter how annoying this is!);
- Your friends (non business development people), who can provide common-sense perspectives uncluttered by either good or bad sales experience; and
- Your coaches in the account, who have a vested interest in your success.

Keep in mind that we don't have to agree with all of their ideas or accept all of their suggestions. We must gather input, cull through the ideas and develop the best possible strategy. In sales, the buck really does stop here!

Tip 102. The Toughest Sale

Sometimes the internal sale is our toughest sale of all, and nowhere is this more true than when we are dealing with a challenging procurement situation. This is true because all of our internal stakeholders have their own unique motivations. The needs of Finance vary depending upon the state of the business; our solution designers want a highly-qualified deal before engaging; and the leadership team may want more opportunities in the pipeline, regardless of the deal's validity. After all, even a bad deal looks pretty good in an otherwise weak pipeline. You, on the other hand, want support for a difficult decision. If you turn down an opportunity to react to a bad deal in order to proactively go after a new opportunity, you know you are exposed—even if your logic is sound.

As we've written in previous Tips, we have different options to consider when dealing with Procurement, from following the rules to walking away to offering a compromise—and many more. After careful consideration, you are ready to proceed, and now need to sell your decision internally.

Of course, nothing is better than possessing the direct and visible support of your manager and other senior executives. If you have this, great! However, just because you have this support doesn't mean your sales effort is over. Get others engaged, do your research and understand the perspectives of the key players on your team. This knowledge is valuable as you build a solid business case that backs up your decision.

To make your case in the most compelling manner, follow the IMPAX "Them-Us-Fit-Action" flow and present your case proactively to the right people on your team!

Tip 103. Shield Yourself

Part of creating and executing your strategy is developing a "personal protection plan." This plan will help shield you from the fallout should things go wrong. There are a number of ways to do this, including:

Utilizing a senior-level executive from your company:

- They are often removed from the day-to-day activities in the account.
- Due to their executive role, they are typically immune from the rules governing sales and account management people.
- They have the power to make decisions many salespeople cannot.
- In many cases, they have the right, interest and inclination to reach out to their senior-level executive counterparts in the account for top-to-top discussions of executive interest.
- They have their own network of senior executive relationships.
- We work for them, sometimes several organizational layers removed, and we have no control over them. Therefore, we are somewhat powerless over their actions.
- We can relate to our organizational peers in the account as our corresponding senior executives do their own thing.

Utilizing a coach within the account who has the power and organizational presence to help us:

- They can influence the decision makers on our behalf.
- They can take the heat when Procurement comes after you.
- They can take responsibility for our actions if we go astray by letting people know they suggested we follow a particular path.

Developing a powerful relationship with the decision maker who recognizes and appreciates your value.

There is no sure thing, and we realize that. If things go wrong, we may get burned. But by giving it some thought ahead of time, we increase the odds that we can come through unscathed (or at least intact).

"Everybody has a plan until they get punched in the mouth."

Mike Tyson

Tip 104. Back it Up

It's not enough to develop our strategy. We also want to optimize our odds for success by preparing a backup plan. After all, no plan is foolproof.

Part of developing a sound strategy is thinking through not just what should work, but what could go wrong and how to react if the worst happens.

It could sound something like this:

"My plan for dealing with the procurement department in this account is to meet with them directly in the near term, before there is a specific opportunity on the table. I will do my research to better understand their role and POSI, and try to identify ways I can help them win. I will also position my role and my organization's sales philosophy, so they know I have to sell the value of our offerings directly to the department where our solutions make an impact. While doing this, I will also search my network to find other contacts outside of Procurement who I can develop into coaches.

Based on my understanding right now, this should be an effective strategy. However, if they try to block me, I will get out of the meeting without agreeing to the block, and I will leverage my COO, who has a strong relationship with their COO, to establish a direct executive relationship."

By creating a primary and backup plan, we are thinking and acting strategically. It's like playing chess. We shouldn't be thinking solely about our next move. We should be thinking several moves ahead.

IMPAX MAXIM

"A good strategy is usually a combination of several."

Tip 105. Get the Word Out

The communication of our plan is a key step we cannot afford to forget. It's essential to inform our team what we are doing and why we are doing it.

Several of the previous Tips focused on how to leverage our team. Now it's time to take their input, determine our plan of action and execute. We still need to close the loop and let the team know our plan. It's incumbent upon us to make sure that everyone is on the same page. Our leaders and teammates need to know, so they don't get blindsided. We need them to know, so we can continue to leverage their knowledge, insights and relationships.

As we communicate to the team how we arrived at the plan and why we decided to do what we did, we also want to share our plan of action. This way, they will have the context they need should they ever be asked. Imagine how they would feel if cornered at an industry association meeting by a person who asked, "Hey, why did your company choose to "no-bid" on our RFP?" The only thing worse than not having an answer is not knowing we chose this course of action in the first place.

It's not just our own team we want to communicate with, either. We want to make sure we keep our coaches in the loop. Remembering that our coaches win when we win, we want to always put them in a position to be successful and not let them be taken by surprise. The better they understand our strategy, the more they can support it and capitalize on it.

Tip 106. Walk Away

As sales professionals, we constantly face challenges in which we have no control, like a global economic recession and desperate competitors who are just trying to survive. We do, however, have control over one thing: how we choose to react to these challenges.

Here's an example. Most of us have responded to an RFP where we knew we had a superior solution and overall value but almost no chance of winning. Why did we respond? We probably believed we needed to so we didn't send the wrong message to the prospect. We don't want them to stop including us in their evaluation process, even if we have little chance of winning. A different strategy is to walk away from the opportunity. Done well, this might get us closer to winning than responding outright. How? By doing these things when we walk away:

- Position your decision at all levels of the buying organization, including with the senior-level decision makers.
- Don't make your decision a personal attack against anyone in the organization.
- Let your frustration show—not because of their convoluted process, but because you feel strongly that you could make a huge difference for them given a fair chance.
- Give some insights to the impact you could make.
- Be honest and tell them you don't feel you could effectively compete given their ground rules.
- Share the conditions under which you would be willing to compete.

Here's how it might sound when you tell a decision maker you aren't going to compete:

"I wanted to let you know of a difficult decision we've made. We have decided not to respond to your RFP or compete for this opportunity. This is frustrating to me, as I believe we have a superior solution that could truly help you drive customer retention to new levels by addressing your system responsiveness issues, thereby helping to hit your RONA target. We have decided not to compete because it seems your RFP criteria and buying process do not provide us the ability to adequately position our value and compete effectively. It would be a waste of everyone's time. If, on the other hand, we had a chance to make a presentation to you and your decision team where we could share our view of the fit between our companies, as well as our RFP response, I believe we could compete effectively. Would that be possible?"

There are a lot of decision makers who would be impressed by a potential supplier with this degree of knowledge, conviction and commitment, and who would want to hear what you have to say. They may just give you the meeting. This demonstrates that there are times when we can take control and improve our ability to compete, even by choosing not to compete.

Real World Application

What would it take for you to walk away?

Consider these questions to determine if you should walk away:

What are the conditions under which you typically succeed?

What are the RFP rules in a current situation?

Which rules/criteria make you feel like you have no shot at winning?

What are your odds of success?

What would it cost you in time/effort/money to respond?

What other reasons could compel you to reply when there is a small chance of winning?

Are you good enough to win given different contacts and rules?

The answers to these questions should provide you with enough information to determine if walking away is worth it.

Think about these questions when considering how to walk away:

Who is the RFP administrator?

Who is the line executive responsible for the opportunity?

How badly is your response needed to validate their vendor grid?

Under what conditions would you agree to participate (e.g. you are guaranteed a finalist presentation)?

Prepare your "script" to deliver to the decision maker about your decision to walk away.

Tip 107. Be a Pro

Does your organization have stated company values? One company we know of lives by these clearly-articulated and often-communicated values:

- Act with integrity and responsibility;
- Respect and recognize each other; and
- Work together to deliver for internal and external customers.

If our companies have stated values, then business development professionals should live by them, especially in the way we interact with our customers and prospects.

When executing our procurement and sales strategy, we want to be able to walk with our heads held high, knowing we are doing things in an honest and ethical manner. This means being honest about our capabilities, not telling "white lies," not disparaging our competitors and generally conducting ourselves as if anything we do might be written about on the front page of our local newspaper—and read by our mothers!

Of course, it's not all black and white. There are gray areas, too. For example, we do not have to divulge our strategy to those who would like to see us fail. We do, however, need to be honest and ethical as we execute this strategy. Not just because it's the right thing to do, but also because we know that "what comes around goes around." If we compromise our values to win a deal, it will come back to haunt us eventually.

IMPAX MAXIM

"There is no substitute for integrity."

One last idea: If our companies don't have stated values, we should consider leading an effort to create some! They can be a unifying focal point for companies and are often appreciated by customers.

Tip 108. Gaining Immunity

We can all get behind the goal of becoming immune to Procurement and gatekeepers!

Can this ever really happen, though? Can we ever be completely safe from the damage that a commoditizing procurement person or an antagonistic evaluator can do to us? The answer probably lies in your experience with your best customer relationships. These are the relationships where:

- You have a strong relationship with senior-level decision makers.
- You have developed a vibrant coach network.
- Your organization and solutions have delivered visible value and have been recognized for it.
- The two companies are interconnected in many ways.
- Your solutions have set the standard for performance.
- The two companies have helped each other in many "out of the box" ways.
- You have regular input into each other's strategic planning process.

Back to the question at hand, "Can we ever be completely immune?" The key word here is "completely." Of course, there are no guarantees. Many things could happen: the decision makers could leave; your coaches retire; your gatekeepers get promoted; the company could be purchased; they could fall into a difficult financial situation and try to save their way to prosperity; etc. Nonetheless, by doing the right things, you can reduce your risks and become nearly "gatekeeper-proof."

Will we eliminate the relationship with Procurement? Probably not, but maybe this should not be our goal. Instead, we could change the nature of the relationship to one of collaboration rather than commoditization.

Real World Application

Consider this question:

What would it take to become immune from Procurement and other gatekeepers in a customer situation?

Exercise:

Select a customer situation where you are in a relatively good position and answer these questions:

What are your strengths?

Who are your strongest coaches?

How strong is your relationship with the decision maker?

How would you describe the solution fit and the business fit?

How is Procurement perceived in the organization?

How would you describe your relationship with Procurement?

Given your answers to these questions, write an action plan that if executed, could put you in a position to be immune from Procurement:

Action Item	Responsibility	Timeframe

Tip 109. Upon Further Review

How can we get better at dealing with Procurement and RFPs and improve our odds of success? One way is to conduct Win/Loss Reviews, where we look at our past deals and learn from them. Here are some questions to ask about each deal:

Loss Reviews:

What was the reason (or reasons) they gave for not selecting us?

Were we involved in the opportunity prior to the RFP?

Did we have any influence on the bid specs?

How effectively did we understand their business direction and needs?

What questions should we have asked but didn't?

What were their rules of engagement?

What was our strategy?

How strong was our coach network?

Did we present to senior-level decision makers (versus submitting via email)?

What are the top three reasons we lost (outsold, price, weak coaching, poor fit, etc.)?

How effectively did we involve the right people from our team (support resources, executives, etc.)?

Did we do everything we could to change the ground rules to our favor?

What would we do differently if we could go back and try again?

Win Reviews:

Are we pleased with the outcome (solution fit, price, etc.)?

What did we do well?

What was the turning point?

What reasons did they give as to why they selected us?

How did we avoid the traps?

What were our critical success factors (good coaching, executive access, support from our leadership team, etc.)?

How did we differentiate ourselves?

What would we replicate in future deals?

By asking these questions, we can gain tremendous insight and ensure our future efforts are more effective.

_____

"You may never know what results come of your action, but if you do nothing there will be no result."

Mahatma Gandhi

Tip 110. Taking the Lead

Throughout this book, "Breaking the Rules" has been the theme of these Tips. Why? Because, as we all know, too many times the rules are made so that value leaders lose. The rise of Procurement is putting immense pressure on value-leading sales organizations that can deliver great value to customers, but can't win price-oriented vendor battles.

We have shared a series of ideas to consider when breaking the rules, and we want to reiterate a couple of key messages: breaking the rules requires courage, and it requires taking action. Breaking the rules isn't easy, but neither is the alternative of playing a game you can't win. Below is an example of this kind of courage. It is an excerpt from an email sent by a sales leader to his team (our client's identity has been hidden to protect his competitive advantage) to encourage the right kind of action:

> **"Our sector is adopting the position that all RFPs that we elect to respond to going forward must be presented to the decision maker in person as a condition of our response. If this is not acceptable to the group organizing the bid, we will 'pass' on the RFP response. Presentations to an 'RFP committee' will not be acceptable, unless the decision maker is present in the meeting. (Again, a decision maker is the person who is responsible for the selection of our company as a service partner.)**
>
> **Additionally, for all non-RFP responses, the business development leader on a given pursuit is required to use the full IMPAX process, including making a business fit presentation to the decision maker at the beginning of a pursuit and then again when the solution is finalized.**
>
> **This position will not be compromised for any customer or prospective customer."**

Courageous? Yes. And smart, too. He and his team are getting the presentation meetings with senior management they need in order to position their value, differentiate themselves from their competition and win.

Tip 111. High Hopes

Never before has the role of sales and business development been more important and more undervalued at the same time! All of the challenges we've laid out in this book are real, and in some cases it's even worse than we've illustrated.

On the other hand, what we do is more important than ever. We have the knowledge, experience, network and creativity to truly help our customers do better business, and the pressure for these companies to perform is incredible.

Although these two points are opposed, should we have reason to hope? Absolutely! If we stick to our guns, the pendulum will eventually start to swing back the other way. In fact, a recent survey by the Consero Group, in partnership with Vantage Partners, seems to back this up.

They found, not surprisingly, that the majority (65%) of CPOs focus on using competitive pressure to get maximum value rather than use collaboration to achieve the same results (35%). The only thing surprising about this is that it's only 65-35!

In the same study, more than half of the respondents agreed that their company pursues short-term savings from suppliers that undermine long-term value. These organizations are understaffed, overworked and the victims of unrealistic expectations. We need to stick to our guns and keep fighting the value battle, and the tide will turn.

IMPAX MAXIM

"There are better days ahead!"

Conclusion

A merchant ship was out on the open sea, when a sailor called down from the crow's nest, "Captain, there's a pirate ship on the horizon!" The captain alerted the crew and asked his first mate, "Bring me my red shirt!" He then led his crew to victory. The next day, the sailor called down, "Captain, there are two pirate ships on the horizon!" Again, he said to his first mate, "Bring me my red shirt!", and again he led them to victory. The men were in awe of their captain, and wondered about his red shirt, so they convinced the first mate to ask the captain why he always wears his red shirt in battle. He tells them it's because if he is wounded, he doesn't want the men to worry, but to fight on bravely to victory. The men are even more impressed upon hearing the story. The next day the sailor calls down to the captain, "Captain, there are 10 pirate ships on the horizon!" The captain then turned to his first mate and said, "Bring me my brown pants!"

It's really tough out there! The disempowerment of business development professionals is one of the most difficult challenges we face in this era of commoditization. The rules that have been put in place so that customers can level the playing field have made it difficult for true sales professionals and value leaders to do what we do best: understand the customer's business and work to create innovative solutions that help them attain critical objectives, implement high priority strategies and address crucial issues. These solutions leverage our value—a combination of our solutions, experience, people, knowledge, processes and future direction.

---

*"Far better is it to dare mighty things, to win
glorious triumphs, even though checkered by
failure, than to rank with those poor spirits
who neither enjoy much nor suffer much,
because they live in the gray twilight that
knows neither victory nor defeat."*

Theodore Roosevelt

We at IMPAX are in the same boat as you. We are out there selling too and face the same challenges. Here is a story about one of our experiences:

We had the opportunity to begin a consulting and training relationship with the U.S. arm of a multinational company. It developed into a fantastic win-win relationship. The client implemented the IMPAX Process to great success due to their talented team and strong leadership. As a result of our mutual success, the suggestion was made that the company consider implementing a global sales process to get the benefit of a common process and language. We thought that was a great idea! Others did too, and someone from corporate thought it would be a good idea to issue an RFP. We didn't think that was such a great idea, but the decision was made.

A person was chosen to lead the RFP effort. He was based in London. They decided to go with five "vendors": IMPAX and four competitors from London, known personally to the administrator. All of the classic rules were instituted: quick response, give us only the prescribed information, follow this format, no contact with anyone during the tender period, etc. Ironically, when the RFP arrived via email, we were in the middle of a leadership development session with the Chief Development Officer of the U.S. team. According to the rules, we shouldn't have even been talking with him and his team.

Out of principle, or stubbornness, we made a list of all the rules so we could visibly break them! Things got interesting when they required our response via email by April 11. We responded by requesting a variance, saying, "Unfortunately, we can't meet the April 11 deadline. However, we will be at a conference with the three global sales executives on April 14 and would be in a great position to present our response at that time." His response was to let everyone know what idiots we were for not playing the game. Meanwhile, we continued working behind the scenes with our coaches, to make sure that we could get our presentation scheduled. We needed the presentation to differentiate IMPAX from the other training companies and position the power of an expanded relationship with us. Fortunately, we were able to present to the decision makers, and we practiced what we preach. We used our own presentation process ("Them-Us-Fit-Action") and focused on a compelling business fit. We also gave them our completed RFP response.

We learned a lot following the presentation. For instance, it turns out that none of our competitors even asked for an opportunity to present. What were they thinking? That their proposals would put them over the top? They were sales training companies! As a client told us, "It's hard to put passion on paper." We also learned that if it were up to the RFP administrator, we would not have been the choice (too expensive). Lastly, we found out that the administrator was a really nice guy who was trying to do the best job he could. It's just that what he wanted and what we wanted were different. He wanted a relatively inexpensive training event, and we wanted to help the company implement a sales and account management process that could help them strengthen their efforts to drive business results. Luckily for us, that's what the decision makers wanted, too.

••••••••••••••••••••••••••••••••••••••

"The last thing we wanted was to partner with someone who was following the rules. We were already doing that and it wasn't working for us. What we needed was a partner who could help us chart a different course. We are truly value leaders and we can't afford to get commoditized. It's up to us to find a way to sell this value. Now, we have found that when we can present to the decision maker with input from good coaches, we are almost unstoppable. When we "mail it in" we are almost always stopped. This is now our strategy, and we're glad that IMPAX broke the rules."

Mike Gardner
Chief Development Officer
Exel

••••••••••••••••••••••••••••••••••••••

What a story. Even with a great client, we can find ourselves being commoditized. The rules are changing, and procurement is on the rise. In many cases, we are disempowered. We are pounding away on a keyboard responding to increasingly unreasonable RFPs, which we will probably lose. That's not why most of us got into business development. We got into it because we loved the customer interaction, loved figuring out how to help solve problems to drive business results and enjoyed compelling the right people. That's motivating. That's fun! That's why we got into this career. We've never heard a rep say, "I got into this profession because I love typing away on an RFP response well into the wee hours, especially when I know I'm going to lose!"

With this disempowerment comes a massive hit on morale and career satisfaction. The very act of "Breaking the Rules" can change all of this. When we are empowered to break the rules and to try something different, our creativity and innovation emerge. Now we are confident again, morale is up, and we can do what we're best at. Now more than ever, we have to remember that this is supposed to be fun, and we're at our best when we are enjoying the hours we put in.

•••••••••••••••••••••••••••••••••••••••

"Sales can be an exciting and rewarding career. The best salespeople are creative, curious and hardworking professionals who love working with a variety of people and making an impact on their customer's business. In my experience, a strong group of these people can set the tone for the entire company. This 'rise of procurement' can take the wind out of the sails of even the best reps and that can ripple through a company. We simply cannot afford to let that happen. We have to push back. The ramifications are too severe. If we cannot charge for our value, how can we employ the people who bring that value to life? We simply have to bend or break the rules, and bring the fun back to sales."

Chris Powell
President
Precyse

•••••••••••••••••••••••••••••••••••••••

Never has this been more important to the profession of sales. The pendulum has swung a long way, and it really is tough out there: We are facing challenges that didn't exist just a few years ago; the instincts we've honed can let us down in this new era; our competition is as desperate as our customers; the short-term view is taking over; many of our customers are trying to save their way to prosperity—and we're stuck in the middle. We're at our best when we are helping customers improve the way they do business, but many don't want that kind of help.

But some do: the senior-level decision makers who are more strategic and can see the bigger picture. We simply have to get to them and compel them. It's our job, and it's the best way to success.

Now is the time to get to work, and that is what we do best! Consider this story.

A group of salespeople were stranded in a hotel during a bad storm and wondered when they would be able to get back on the road to make some sales calls. They asked everyone who came in how bad the roads were. One wise person said, "Well, that depends. Are you on salary or commission?"

There are so many things we can do to improve our situation ... if we just take action!

Think about a national sales meeting you've attended. Have they ever trotted some rep up to the stage and said, "Here's Tom. He had a bad year, but it wasn't his fault. He did everything right but those RFPs just weren't fair. Let's give him a nice round of applause along with this big bonus check!"

That doesn't happen. There really is no glory for a victim. The people running up to the stage, high fiving the crowd on their way up, are the people who've found a way to make it happen. The glory, the admiration and the money all go to the people who help their customers succeed no matter how challenging the obstacles.

IMPAX MAXIM

"There is no glory for a victim!"

Real World Application

Consider this situation faced by an IMPAX client:

They had done some analysis to find that when they followed the customer's rules and responded to RFPs their aggregated hit rate was 26%

They continued their analysis and found that when they developed a network of 3 or more coaches, got to the real decision maker and made a presentation that follows the IMPAX Them-Us-Fit-Action flow, their hit rate was 75%

What would you do?

What did they do?

They did a number of things:

1. They redesigned their RFP assessment worksheet and featured activities like:

    - Amount of customer knowledge;
    - Strength of their coach network; and
    - Ability to access the decision maker.

2. They strengthened their networking skills and focused on developing a strong network of coaches in every account they were pursuing.

3. They emphasized the importance of decision maker access from the beginning of the cycle.

4. They mandated this policy: "We will no longer respond to any RFP without first requesting an opportunity to present our response to the decision maker."

Oh yeah, they won a lot, too. They changed the rules, created real competitive advantage and aggressively sold their value. You can, too!

Appendix A
RFP ASSESSMENT GRID

<u>RFP Assessment Ranking</u>

Criteria/Weighting	Score
1.	
2.	
3.	
4.	
5.	
6.	
7.	
8.	
9.	
10.	
Grand Total	

Appendix B
INFLUENCE GRID

Influence Grid

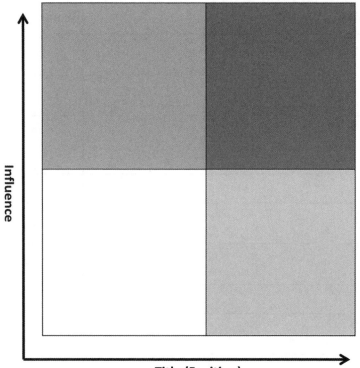

Appendix C
POSI GRID

POSI Grid

Profile (As Is)	**Objectives** (To Be)
Issues (Barriers & Concerns)	**Strategies** (How?)

Appendix D

SAMPLE IMPAX BUSINESS FIT PRESENTATION

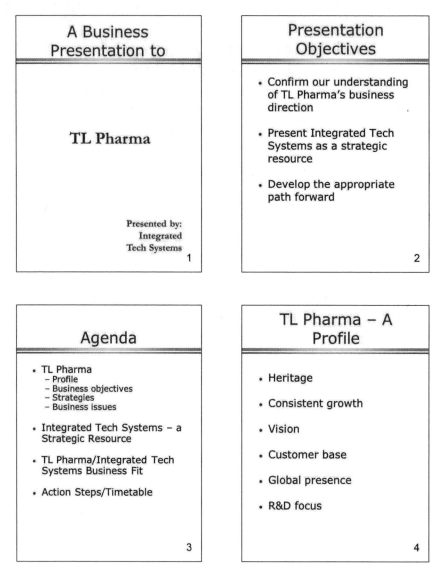

A Business Presentation to

TL Pharma

Presented by:
Integrated
Tech Systems

1

Presentation Objectives

- Confirm our understanding of TL Pharma's business direction

- Present Integrated Tech Systems as a strategic resource

- Develop the appropriate path forward

2

Agenda

- TL Pharma
  - Profile
  - Business objectives
  - Strategies
  - Business issues

- Integrated Tech Systems – a Strategic Resource

- TL Pharma/Integrated Tech Systems Business Fit

- Action Steps/Timetable

3

TL Pharma – A Profile

- Heritage

- Consistent growth

- Vision

- Customer base

- Global presence

- R&D focus

4

Appendix D (continued)
SAMPLE IMPAX BUSINESS FIT PRESENTATION

TL Pharma –
Business Objectives

- Achieve growth targets
- Expand U.S. market share
- Strengthen global presence
- Improve operational efficiencies
- Increase profitability

5

TL Pharma –
Strategies

- Grow by acquisition
- Position technical expertise
- Leverage quality certification
- Invest in training & development
- Utilize outside resources

6

TL Pharma –
Business Issues

- Competitive landscape
- Market volatility
- Increasing costs
- Time to market
- Inventory levels

7

Integrated Tech Systems –
A Strategic Resource

- Mission statement
- Market leadership
- Provider of business solutions
- Track record of innovation
- Business/technology alliances
- Long-term partnerships

8

Appendix D (continued)
SAMPLE IMPAX BUSINESS FIT PRESENTATION

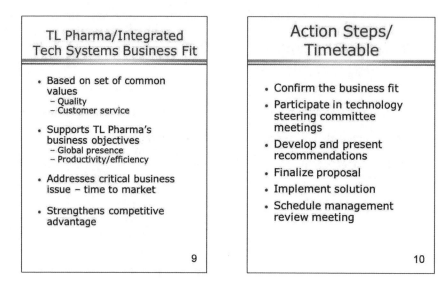

TL Pharma/Integrated Tech Systems Business Fit

- Based on set of common values
  - Quality
  - Customer service
- Supports TL Pharma's business objectives
  - Global presence
  - Productivity/efficiency
- Addresses critical business issue – time to market
- Strengthens competitive advantage

9

Action Steps/ Timetable

- Confirm the business fit
- Participate in technology steering committee meetings
- Develop and present recommendations
- Finalize proposal
- Implement solution
- Schedule management review meeting

10

Appendix E

SAMPLE IMPAX RFP FINALIST PRESENTATION

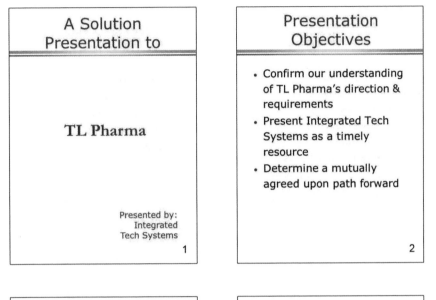

A Solution Presentation to

TL Pharma

Presented by:
Integrated
Tech Systems

1

Presentation Objectives

- Confirm our understanding of TL Pharma's direction & requirements
- Present Integrated Tech Systems as a timely resource
- Determine a mutually agreed upon path forward

2

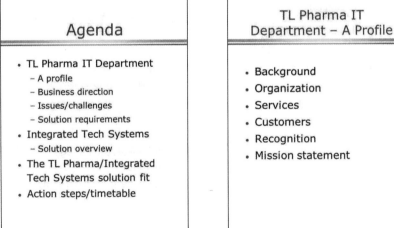

Agenda

- TL Pharma IT Department
  - A profile
  - Business direction
  - Issues/challenges
  - Solution requirements
- Integrated Tech Systems
  - Solution overview
- The TL Pharma/Integrated Tech Systems solution fit
- Action steps/timetable

3

TL Pharma IT Department – A Profile

- Background
- Organization
- Services
- Customers
- Recognition
- Mission statement

4

Appendix E (continued)

SAMPLE IMPAX RFP FINALIST PRESENTATION

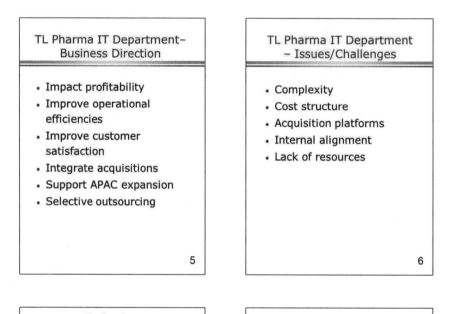

TL Pharma IT Department–
Business Direction

- Impact profitability
- Improve operational
  efficiencies
- Improve customer
  satisfaction
- Integrate acquisitions
- Support APAC expansion
- Selective outsourcing

5

TL Pharma IT Department
– Issues/Challenges

- Complexity
- Cost structure
- Acquisition platforms
- Internal alignment
- Lack of resources

6

Solution
Requirements

- Seamless integration
- Platform consistency
- AI certification
- Flexibility
- Industry experience

7

Integrated Tech Systems –
A Strategic Resource

- Mission statement
- Market leadership
- Provider of business
  solutions
- Track record of innovation
- Business/technology
  alliances
- Long-term partnerships

8

Appendix E (continued)

SAMPLE IMPAX RFP FINALIST PRESENTATION

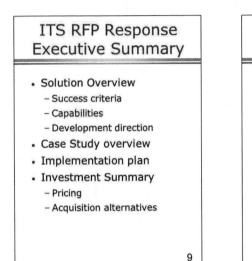

ITS RFP Response Executive Summary

- Solution Overview
  - Success criteria
  - Capabilities
  - Development direction
- Case Study overview
- Implementation plan
- Investment Summary
  - Pricing
  - Acquisition alternatives

9

TL Pharma/ITS Solution Fit

- Meets and exceeds technical requirements
  - Platform
  - Certification
- Provides unique capabilities
  - 6GL
- Provides critical resources
  - APAC expertise
  - Industry references

10

Action Steps/ Timetable

- Conduct system demo — Today
- Identify and address open questions — Today
- Gain commitment — Today
- Schedule reference site visit — Today
- Conduct reference site visit — 30 days
- Conduct implementation planning meeting — 30 days

11

Appendix F

SAMPLE IMPAX BUSINESS RELATIONSHIP REVIEW PRESENTATION

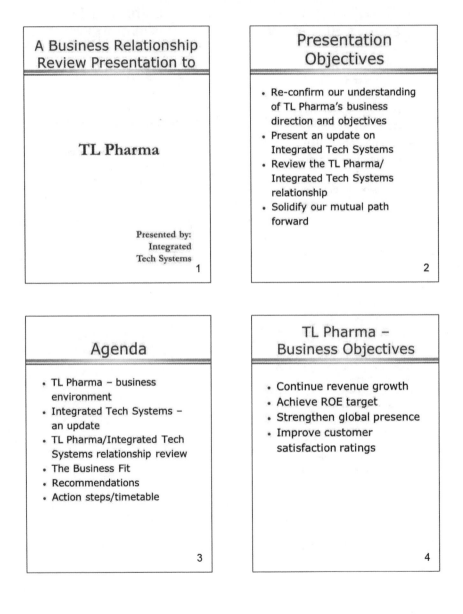

A Business Relationship Review Presentation to

TL Pharma

Presented by:
Integrated
Tech Systems

1

Presentation Objectives

- Re-confirm our understanding of TL Pharma's business direction and objectives
- Present an update on Integrated Tech Systems
- Review the TL Pharma/ Integrated Tech Systems relationship
- Solidify our mutual path forward

2

Agenda

- TL Pharma – business environment
- Integrated Tech Systems – an update
- TL Pharma/Integrated Tech Systems relationship review
- The Business Fit
- Recommendations
- Action steps/timetable

3

TL Pharma – Business Objectives

- Continue revenue growth
- Achieve ROE target
- Strengthen global presence
- Improve customer satisfaction ratings

4

Appendix F (continued)

SAMPLE IMPAX BUSINESS RELATIONSHIP
REVIEW PRESENTATION

TL Pharma - Strategies

- Grow by acquisition
- Reduce fixed costs
- Implement TQM process
- Increase R&D spending
- Rollout organization changes

5

TL Pharma – Issues

- Business
  - New market competition
  - Government regulations

- Technology
  - Escalating costs
  - Incompatible platforms
  - Specific expertise

6

Integrated Tech Systems – An Update

- Segment focus
- Market leadership
- Acquisition of EU partner
- Track record of innovation
- Business/technology alliances - SEL
- Long-term partnerships

7

TL Pharma/Integrated Tech Systems Relationship Review

- Activities
  - International rollout
  - Outsourcing of APAC facility
  - Joint TQM training
  - Implementation of annual metrics
  - Cross-staffing

8

Appendix F (continued)
SAMPLE IMPAX BUSINESS RELATIONSHIP REVIEW PRESENTATION

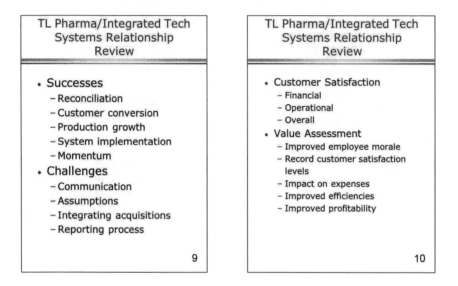

TL Pharma/Integrated Tech Systems Relationship Review

- Successes
  - Reconciliation
  - Customer conversion
  - Production growth
  - System implementation
  - Momentum
- Challenges
  - Communication
  - Assumptions
  - Integrating acquisitions
  - Reporting process

9

TL Pharma/Integrated Tech Systems Relationship Review

- Customer Satisfaction
  - Financial
  - Operational
  - Overall
- Value Assessment
  - Improved employee morale
  - Record customer satisfaction levels
  - Impact on expenses
  - Improved efficiencies
  - Improved profitability

10

TL Pharma/Integrated Tech Systems Business Fit

- Leverages mutual priority on:
  - Innovation
  - Relationships
- Supports critical business objective – profitability
- Addresses priority business issues:
  - Outsourcing
  - Global expansion

11

Recommendations/ Action Steps

- Confirm business fit — Today
- Schedule meeting to develop implementation plan based on recommendations — Today
- Present LATAM outsourcing recommendation — Today
- Review joint TQM project results — ASAP
- Conduct annual business review — 1/15
- Schedule next relationship review meeting — Today

12

About the Authors

Co-authors and IMPAX Corporation Co-Presidents Mark Shonka and Dan Kosch have each tallied more than 25 years of experience in direct sales, sales management, and sales consulting and training. IMPAX, a leading global sales performance improvement company, is committed to helping clients improve their sales, account management, channel management and sales leadership efforts to drive business results. IMPAX has worked with thousands of sales professionals in the field and the classroom around the world.

Shonka and Kosch are highly sought-after authorities on a range of sales topics including selling value, strategic account selling, strategic account management, sales leadership and dealing with procurement. With names like IBM, DHL, DuPont, American Express, Pfizer, US Bank, GE Healthcare, Dell, McKesson and Volvo, the authors' client list reflects some of the world's leading sales organizations.

Dan and Mark have also authored the best-selling book, <u>Beyond Selling Value</u>, published by Kaplan Publishing.

If you would like more information about IMPAX and about how we can help your company sell value, please contact us at:

IMPAX Corporation

Toll free: 800-457-4727
Office: 203-222-1900
Fax: 203-222-8445

E-mail: info@impaxcorp.com
Website: www.impaxcorp.com